Maryland's
Catoctin Mountain Parks

Maryland's
Catoctin Mountain Parks

An Interpretive Guide
to
Catoctin Mountain Park
and
Cunningham Falls State Park

by

John Means

The McDonald & Woodward Publishing Company
Blacksburg, Virginia
1995

The McDonald & Woodward Publishing Company
Guides to the American Landscape series

Maryland's Catoctin Mountain Parks
An Interpretive Guide to Catoctin Mountain Park and Cunningham
Falls State Park

© 1995 by The McDonald & Woodward Publishing Company
P. O. Box 10308, Blacksburg, Virginia 24062-0308

All rights reserved. First printing September 1995.
Composition by Rowan Mountain, Inc., Blacksburg, Virginia.
Printed by McNaughton & Gunn, Inc., Saline, Michigan.

04 03 02 01 00 99 98 97 96 95   10 9 8 7 6 5 4 3 2 1

Library of Congress Cataloging-in-Publication Data

Means, John, 1944–

    Maryland's Catoctin Mountain parks : an interpretive guide to
Catoctin Mountain Park and Cunningham Falls State Park / by
John Means.
      p. cm. -- (The McDonald & Woodward Publishing
Company guides to the American landscape series)
    Includes bibliographical references and index.
    ISBN 0-939923-38-6 (alk. paper)
    1. Catoctin Mountain Park (Md.)--Guidebooks. 2.
Cunningham Falls State Park (Md.)--Guidebooks. I. Title.
II. Series: McDonald & Woodward guide to the American
landscape.
F187.F8M43   1995
917.52'87--dc20   95-31051
                                              CIP

Table of Contents

Table of Contents

Introduction

Catoctin Mountain Park and Cunningham Falls State Park are located side by side on approximately 10,000 acres of mountain land in western Maryland. The parks occupy the easternmost ridge of the Blue Ridge Province. Known as the Catoctin Mountains, this ridge has elevations generally in the range of 1,600 to 1,700 feet, and it rises abruptly from north to south more than 1,200 feet above the adjacent Frederick Valley.

Catoctin Mountain Park is managed by the National Park Service and is located to the north of Maryland Route 77; Cunningham Falls State Park is managed by the Maryland Forest, Park, and Wildlife Service and is located to the south of Route 77 (Figures 1 and 2).

Figure 1. The entrance to the parks from the west is through a tunnel of trees that is beautiful during all seasons.

The area covered by the two parks is notable for a variety of features. The unique geology of the Catoctins opens windows not only to the ancient history of the earth but also to the intermediate history—which includes the formation of the Appalachian mountains—and to the more recent events of the Ice Age. The streams and falls that are a part of this geologic history are excellent for fishing, study or meditation. The regenerated forests offer opportunities for the study of ecological concepts and wildlife habitats. Finally, the sites related to the 19th century iron industry and to the New Deal programs of the 1930s provide interest to the student of American history.

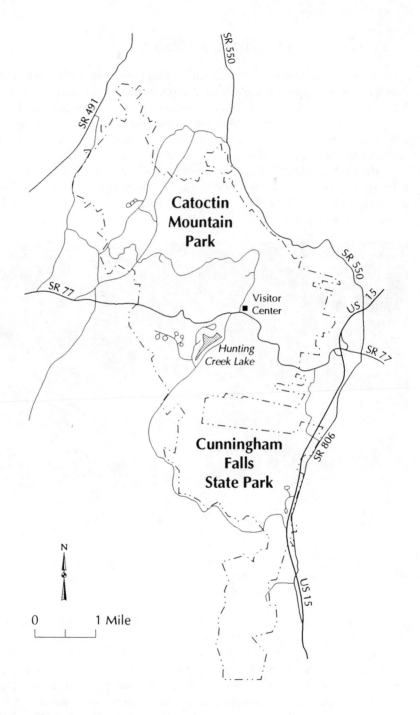

Figure 2. The parks are located north and south of Maryland Route 77, with Hunting Creek Lake and the Visitor Center centrally located.

Table 1. A Statistical Synopsis of Catoctin Mountain Park (CMP) and Cunningham Falls State Park (CFSP)

Area:	10,211 acres total. CMP: 5,765 acres. CFSP: 4,446 acres (3,500 acres are state-designated wildlands).
Roads:	About 14 miles of paved roads lie within the parks' boundaries.
Maximum Elevation: .	1,880 feet
Minimum Elevation: .	480 feet (near Catoctin Furnace)
Scenic Overlooks:	Seven. These are accessible only by walking trails.
Trails:	Over 25 miles; several interpretive; two accessible to persons with disabilities; horse trails.
Streams:	Owens, Big Hunting and Little Hunting creeks; numerous tributaries.
Lake:	Hunting Creek Lake: 44 acres, 255 million gallons.
Fishing:	Lake and streams, with some restricted to catch-and-return.
Hunting:	Only on 3,500 acres of wildlands in CFSP.
Overnight Facilities: ..	CFSP: Two campgrounds. CMP: One campground; rustic cabins for rent.
Swimming:	CFSP: Two beach areas at lake.
Boating:	Launching ramp at lake; electric motors less than 1 hp; canoe and aquacycle rental near beach area.
Picnic areas:	CFSP: two areas; snack bar near lake. CMP: two areas and scattered tables.
Activities:	Interpretive programs, hikes, seminars, demonstrations.
Historical Areas:	CFSP: Catoctin Furnace. CMP: Sawmill, Charcoal and Whiskey Still Trails.
Winter Activities:	Cross-country skiing and sledding.
Park Established:	1936, as Catoctin Demonstration Area. 1954, division into two parks.
Annual Visitation:	CFSP: over 900,000 annually. CMP: about 800,000 annually.

For the heavily populated Washington-Baltimore area, some 60 miles to the east (Figure 3), these two parks are the closest sanctuary of undeveloped, protected mountain land. The wooded terrain includes over 25 miles of trails, where the hiker can temporarily escape the trappings of civilization and experience spectacular vistas.

Figure 3. The parks are close to several large cities and to major interstate routes.

This mountain land, with a man-made lake of over 40 acres, offers a variety of recreational opportunities (Figure 4): picnicking, swimming, fishing, hunting, hiking, cabin or tent camping, cross-country skiing, horseback riding trails, sailing and lake canoeing. Numerous self-guided, short interpretive trails offer the chance to walk while learning about natural habitat or human history. Most picnic areas and some trails are accessible to persons with disabilities. Cunningham Falls—a beautiful cascade of 78 feet, the highest waterfall in Maryland—is a popular and easily accessible sight (Figure 5). Several paved roads throughout the parks provide lovely forest drives. The Catoctin Mountain Park Visitor Center offers information, exhibits and a small book store (Figure 7).

Figure 4. Hunting Creek Lake has two beach areas.

Figure 5. Cunningham Falls—a beautiful place to visit.

Figure 6. Cunningham Falls in winter.

Figure 7. Catoctin Mountain Park Visitor Center has exhibits and a book store.

The Catoctin Mountains have not always been so beautiful. In 1935, when the National Park Service acquired the 10,000 acres, most of the trees were about the size of a fence post. The forest had been exhausted from 200 years of logging, of clear-cutting for the iron industry, and of bark-stripping for the tanning industry. Originally called the Catoctin Recreational Demonstration Area, the parks have indeed been a demonstration of how land protection and management by both federal and state agencies can allow a devastated area to return to its natural condition as a mature eastern hardwood climax forest.

Today each park draws almost a million visitors per year; yet the parks seldom seem congested or crowded. Together, the two parks offer a multifaceted invitation to leave the confinement of home, pull away from the heavy traffic and enjoy a refreshing visit to the beautiful Catoctin Mountains.

Origin of the Name Catoctin

The traditional belief is that the name *Catoctin* came from an Indian people, the Kittoctins, who once lived near the Potomac River at the foot of the mountains. However, one writer notes that the Algonquian Indians gave the name *Catoctin* to the ridges and streams of their favorite hunting grounds.

Possible meanings for *Catoctin* are "the place of many deer," "the old hill or mountain," and "speckled mountain," all of which still apply to the area.

Section I

The Geology, Biology and History of Catoctin Mountain Park and Cunningham Falls State Park

Geologic Structure and History

Regional Geologic Setting

Catoctin Mountain Park and adjoining Cunningham Falls State Park comprise over 10,000 acres of Catoctin Mountain, a ridge-shaped mountain that extends fifty miles from Emmitsburg, Maryland, to Leesburg, Virginia. In northern Maryland, Catoctin Mountain is 2 to 4 miles wide, with ridges up to 1,900 feet in elevation. In southern Frederick County, Maryland, and in northern Virginia, the ridge is less than 1 mile wide and elevations average 1,000 feet.

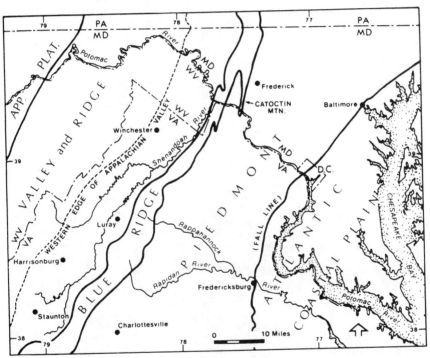

Figure 8. Physiographic provinces of the Middle Atlantic region and southcentral Pennsylvania (from Conners, 1988).

The Blue Ridge Province, a northeast-oriented series of generally linear ridges, stretches over 500 miles from Pennsylvania to Georgia and marks the eastern edge of the Appalachian Mountains. Catoctin Mountain forms the easternmost portion of the Blue Ridge Province of Maryland and Virginia (Figure 8). The western portion of the Blue Ridge in Maryland is South Mountain, which loosely marks the boundary of Frederick and Washington counties.

11

To the west of the Blue Ridge and parallel to it is the Valley and Ridge Province, an alternating series of valleys and ridges. A portion of this series, the Hagerstown Valley and the South Mountain ridge above it, is geologically related to Catoctin Mountain by events that go back over a half-billion years.

East of Catoctin Mountain and easily visible from some of its higher points is the Piedmont Province, a gently rolling area that is markedly lower than the mountains—by about 1,200 feet. In fact, if Catoctin Mountain is viewed from a point several miles to the east, the ridge appears to rise abruptly from a relatively flat area (Figure 9). About 200 million years ago this area was downfaulted into a huge trough, to be filled later with material that eroded from the mountains, which were much higher in former times.

Figure 9. The area from camera position to the Catoctin Mountains is a huge downfaulted trough, filled for millions of years with material eroded from ancient, much higher mountains.

Catoctin Mountain or Catoctin Mountains?

Often the name "Catoctin Mountains" is used. This plural usage seems to designate the general area of the two parks, along with various knobs and high points on the northeast-to-southwest trending ridge that lies west of the Frederick Valley. High points in the "Catoctin Mountains" include, to the northeast of the parks: Piney Mountain (1,724') and Round Top (1,702'); within Catoctin Mountain Park: Thurmont Vista (1,502') and Chimney Rock (1,400'); within Cunningham Falls State Park: Cat Rock (1560') and Bobs Hill (1,747'); and to the south, the mountaintop location of the former Hamburg Lookout Tower (1,623'). Note that within the "Catoctin Mountains" there is no high point or mountaintop called "Catoctin Mountain."

Catoctin Mountain (singular) is a term used by geographers and geologists to refer to the 50-mile-long by 2- to 4-mile-wide ridge that runs from Leesburg, Virginia, to Emmitsburg, Maryland. This singular usage seems to be based on the resistant metavolcanic and quartzite geologic structure of this ridge—just as the term South Mountain is used to refer to the quartzite-topped ridge eight miles to the west in Maryland and Pennsylvania. Geologists designate Catoctin Mountain as the easternmost portion of the Blue Ridge Province of Maryland and northern Virginia; they also refer to it as the eastern flank or limb of the highly eroded Blue Ridge Anticlinorium (called the South Mountain Anticlinorium in Maryland)—an anticlinorium being a large, regionally-sized fold or upwarping in the earth's crust.

The quadrangle topographic maps of the United States Geological Survey use the labels variously. On the Blue Ridge Summit quad, "Catoctin Mountain" labels the highest area of Catoctin Mountain Park. However, on the Catoctin Furnace quad, which maps the area to the south of Hunting Creek, "Catoctin Mountain" is written across the southeast-to-northwest ridge.

In everyday usage, one would probably not say, "I climbed Catoctin Mountain," but instead might say, "I climbed Bobs Hill in the Catoctin Mountains."

Geologic Time

Every landscape, be it hill, valley or prairie, is determined by its past and present underlying rock structure. Even though the same geologic laws have applied throughout the long history of the earth, terrains are in constant change. The rocks that today are outcrops in the Catoctin Mountains were a sea bottom or a lava flow in the distant geologic past.

Conceptualizing geologic time can be a staggering task. The age of the earth is estimated at 4.6 billion years. If we fit earth history into one calendar year and consider the present to be the end of the year—midnight of

13

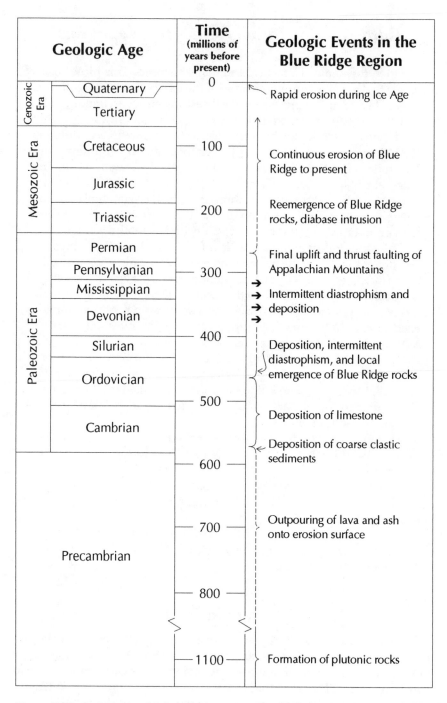

Geologic Age		Time (millions of years before present)	Geologic Events in the Blue Ridge Region
Cenozoic Era	Quaternary	0	Rapid erosion during Ice Age
	Tertiary		
Mesozoic Era	Cretaceous	100	Continuous erosion of Blue Ridge to present
	Jurassic		
	Triassic	200	Reemergence of Blue Ridge rocks, diabase intrusion
Paleozoic Era	Permian		Final uplift and thrust faulting of Appalachian Mountains
	Pennsylvanian	300	
	Mississippian		Intermittent diastrophism and deposition
	Devonian		
	Silurian	400	Deposition, intermittent diastrophism, and local emergence of Blue Ridge rocks
	Ordovician		
	Cambrian	500	Deposition of limestone
		600	Deposition of coarse clastic sediments
Precambrian		700	Outpouring of lava and ash onto erosion surface
		800	
		1100	Formation of plutonic rocks

Figure 10. Geologic time scale, showing approximate, estimated times of important Appalachian and Catoctin events (after Gathright, 1976, and Schirk, 1980).

December 31st—the oldest rocks that we know of date from about mid-March. The greenstone rock that forms Cunningham Falls, one of the older exposed rock formations in the country, dates from late October (about 600 million years ago). Land plants appeared in late November, dinosaurs in mid-December, and man-like creatures during the evening of December 31st. The Ice Age, which was responsible for creating the stone-strewn slopes of the Catoctin Mountains, ended about a minute before midnight on the 31st (about 10,000 years ago). About a quarter of a second before midnight, the federal government acquired the land for the park (1935).

Geologic time is classified into particular periods, and most rock can be dated so that its time of formation is associated with one of those periods (Figure 10). Geologic events, such as lava flows or movements resulting from faults (fractures in rock) are also dated by these periods. For example, most of the rock visible in the Catoctin Mountains dates from Precambrian or from Cambrian times (500 million years or more ago). Why are no "younger" rocks to be found? They were once present, lying on top of what we see today and making the Catoctins many times higher in elevation, but hundreds of millions of years of exposure to rain, running water, wind and ice have caused thousands of feet of rock to be eroded.

The Appalachian Mountains, of which the Catoctins form part of the eastern boundary, are about 250 million years old. Geologically speaking, they are old and worn down. By contrast, the Himalayas, with an average elevation about 15 times that of the Catoctins, are only about 20 million years old. The Rockies, about seven times higher than the Catoctins, are about 60 million years old.

The Rocks of the Catoctins

Rock is categorized according to the manner in which it was formed, and there are three basic types.

1. **Igneous rocks** are formed by the cooling and hardening of molten rock. If the solidification occurs beneath the earth's surface, the rock is called intrusive igneous. A couple of thousand feet below the Catoctins lies an intrusive granite basement rock that is over one billion years old.

If molten rock reaches the surface, it is called lava. Lava cools and hardens into extrusive igneous rock. The green Catoctin metabasalt (greenstone) of the western half of the parks originated as an ancient lava flow that was probably over 2,000 feet thick in places.

2. **Sedimentary rocks** are formed from the compacting and cementing of sediments, such as gravel, sand, silt or clay. Most sediments are deposited by rivers onto offshore ocean or inland sea bottoms. There they accumulate to a great thickness that compacts the sediment particles as the minerals in the water cement them into rock. Sandstone forms in this way

from sand-sized particles, shale from smaller clay-sized particles, and limestone from particle remains of shells and marine skeletons.

Limestones were involved in the formation of the Catoctins, but they have long since eroded away—even though their related remnants now make up the Hagerstown and Frederick valleys. Sandstones and shales were also present, but their character has been altered through a process known as metamorphism.

3. **Metamorphic rocks** are formed when igneous or sedimentary rocks are subjected to the stresses of heat and pressure, usually deep within the earth. The parent rock undergoes change in character and appearance.

The Weverton Formation is a sandstone, part of which has been metamorphosed into a harder, more highly weather-resistant rock called quartzite. High places in the eastern halves of the parks—Cat Rock, Chimney Rock, Wolf Rock, Bobs Hill—are outcrops of the "ridge-forming" Weverton (Figure 11). Several miles to the west, in Washington County, South Moun-

Figure 11. The middle member of the Weverton Formation is a hard quartzite known as the "ledge-maker" member because it is more resistant to weathering than rocks of other formations that adjoin it. The ledge-maker rock outcrop at the top of the far hill is Chimney Rock.

tain is topped by this same highly resistant Weverton formation. Geologists believe that the two were once connected as part of a great mountain.

In the western halves of the parks, the Catoctin metabasalt formation is the bedrock of Hog Rock, Cunningham Falls and the upper Hunting Creek drainage. Metabasalt is metamorphosed igneous rock, which is also highly resistant to weathering (Figure 12).

Figure 12. The Catoctin metabasalt of Hog Rock is visible in the foreground. Along the distant ridge from left to right (northwest to southeast) are Wolf Rock (barely visible), the "point" of Chimney Rock—both of the Weverton "ledge-maker" quartzite—and the gap carved by Hunting Creek.

Another formation, the Loudoun, lies between the Weverton and the Catoctin formations on the slope to the east of Park Central and Catoctin Hollow Roads. Part of it is composed of conglomerate, a sedimentary rock of irregularly sized gravel, and another part of phyllite, which is metamorphosed shale (Figure 13).

Because the Loudoun is less resistant to weathering than the Weverton or the Catoctin, it has worn away more quickly to create a hollow or valley between the two hills of more resistant rocks. Today, Park Central Road follows part of this valley as it climbs to the north from the Visitor Center, and Catoctin Hollow Road follows another part that climbs to the south.

A geologic map of a state or region gives a top view or aerial representation of the particular rock type that forms the underlying bedrock. The accompanying map outlines where the rocks discussed above, and others, occur as bedrock in the Catoctin Mountains and in the adjacent Frederick Valley (Figure 14).

Figure 13. Tilted beds of the Loudon phyllite are visible just a couple of hundred feet east of the Visitor Center parking lot. The right side of this photograph lies to the southeast, and the rock layers dip (or tilt) in that direction.

Plate Tectonics

Many of the processes that create igneous, sedimentary and metamorphic rock are initiated by the movements and interactions of about a dozen large plates, pieces of the earth's outermost crust. These plates have been changing position, shape and size for the last 2.5 billion years.

Their movement is very slow, only a few inches per year, but the results are dramatic because of the immense size of the plates and the great length of geologic time. If two plates collide, horizontal beds of rocks can be compressed, folded and shoved up to high elevations. For example, the Himalayas resulted from a collision of two plates.

If two plates pull apart, great low places can result, such as the Dead Sea Valley or the basin of the Atlantic Ocean. Sometimes this pulling apart, or rifting, results in the flow of hot, molten lava up through the slowly opening cracks.

The Appalachian Mountains and the mountains in northwestern Africa and western Europe were all formed by a series of collisions of several plates over 250 million years ago (mya)—when all of the continents moved together to form the supercontinent Pangaea (Figure 15). Ever since then, the plates have spread apart at the rate of 1 to 2 inches per year. The Atlantic Ocean continues to widen at this rate.

Both the collisions and the subsequent rifting had dramatic effects on the present structure and appearance of the Catoctins.

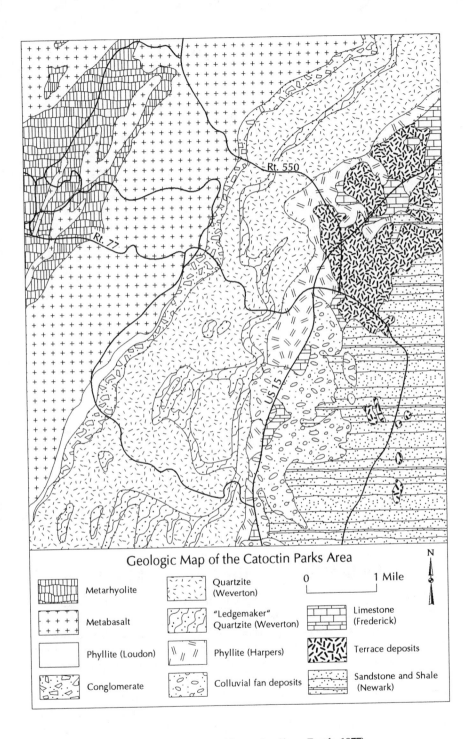

Figure 14. Geologic map of the Catoctin Mountains (from Fauth, 1977).

Geologic Map of the Catoctin Parks Area

Metarhyolite	Quartzite (Weverton)	Limestone (Frederick)
Metabasalt	"Ledgemaker" Quartzite (Weverton)	Terrace deposits
Phyllite (Loudon)	Phyllite (Harpers)	Sandstone and Shale (Newark)
Conglomerate	Colluvial fan deposits	

0   1 Mile

N

Figure 15. Pangaea, the supercontinent assembled over 200 million years ago. Collisions of Eurasia and Africa with North America folded and compressed the land into the Appalachian Mountains (from Olson, 1990).

Geologic History of the Catoctin Mountains

The geologic history of the Appalachian Mountains is long and complex. It involves a series of mountain-building episodes (orogenies), during which the land was compressed, folded and uplifted by collisions of continent-sized plates. Between the orogenies were long periods of erosion, when the mountains were slowly worn down by the weather and reduced in elevation—a process that is still going on today. The sediments eroding from these mountains were deposited offshore in two places: to the east, offshore, in multiple layers at the bottom of the sea; and to the west, in thick wedges of sediment in inland seas that once covered parts of the eastern United States. The final plate collision, or orogeny, uplifted these undersea rock layers into lofty mountains.

The Grenville Orogeny

Over one billion years ago, the continent of North America was about half the size that it is today. Collision with another ancient tectonic plate along the east coast resulted in the Grenville Orogeny, which produced tall mountains that had large intrusions of granitic rock deep within them.

Then, for hundreds of millions of years, these mountains were eroded and reduced in elevation. The resulting landscape was one on which the unearthed granitic crests were about 2,000 feet above the valleys. Because plants and animals did not yet exist, the slopes were probably barren rock on the upper parts and weathered rock debris on the lower parts.

This eroded, uneven terrain was to become the underlying, buried foundation for the layers of rock that today make up the Catoctins. In the Catoctins the ancient and highly eroded Grenville Mountain rock lies about 2,000 feet below the surface, but this core, or basement rock, of the Blue Ridge Province can be seen at the surface in Shenandoah National Park to the south.

Catoctin Volcanism

Approximately 800 to 600 mya, separation of tectonic plates brought about two important results: the opening of the ancient Iapetus Ocean to the east of North America, and crustal extension on land. The resultant strain on the granitic rock caused large blocks of rock to slide downward and fissures or dikes to open. Through these oozed massive volumes of very hot molten lava from below (Figures 16-1 and 17-1). Eventually named the Catoctin Formation, this extrusive volcanic formation is today exposed in mountainous ridges from southern Virginia to south-central Pennsylvania.

There were several episodes—covering tens of millions of years—of alternating lava flows and volcanic ash falls. The stack of sheet-like solidified lava and ash reached maximum thicknesses of about 2,000 feet and formed an extensive lava plain. Because of these great thicknesses, some of the barren granite hilltops were buried beneath the lava plain, but to the west a range of granitic mountains still existed (Figure 17-1).

The lavas that solidified in the Catoctins are of two different mineral or chemical compositions: basalt and rhyolite. Both were later metamorphosed and are referred to collectively as the Catoctin metavolcanics formation. The metabasalt is visible in the park today as greenstone, and the metarhyolite as a dark blue or grey rock. This metavolcanic formation underlies all of the two parks but is exposed at the surface only in the western half, generally northwest of Catoctin Hollow Road.

Paleozoic Subsidence and Deposition

As the volcanism decreased, the southeastern edge of the continent began a lengthy and gradual subsidence, and the growing Iapetus Ocean

21

advanced part way onto the sinking continent from the east. For tens of millions of years—until about 550 mya—thousands of feet of sediment were eroded from the granite and basalt mountains to the west and deposited as mud, sand and quartz pebbles on top of the lower areas of the lava plain, which was now submerged offshore. These deposits resembled the alluvial fans and plains found in desert areas, where a stream flowing down from the mountains drops its sediment load when it reaches a flat area and its velocity slows. The deposits later became the conglomerate and phyllite members of the Loudoun Formation and the sandstones and quartzites of the Weverton Formation. Both of these formations were later uplifted and are visible today in the parks.

General land subsidence relative to the ocean continued, and as stream and river systems were submerged, lagoons and bogs became the primary depositional environment. These quiet-water areas were protected from ocean turbulence by offshore sandbars and barrier islands. Here were dropped the sandy muds and clays that later became the phyllite and sandstone of the Harpers Formation, visible today in the easternmost portions of the parks.

Subsidence continued over millions of years, and as the Loudoun, Weverton and Harpers deposits sank further beneath the water to undergo compaction and cementation into rock, the depositional environment became that of beaches and offshore bars—resembling today's coastal and tidewater areas of North Carolina, Virginia and Maryland. These white and gray sands later became the Antietam quartzite, which is not present today in the parks but is a part of their geologic history. Collectively these four formations—Loudoun, Weverton, Harpers and Antietam, from oldest to youngest—are called the Chilhowee Group.

The continuing subsidence and westward encroachment of the Iapetus Ocean placed these former coastal areas under deep offshore waters (Figures 16-2 and 17-2). Then, for tens of millions of years—until about 450 mya—biological and chemical carbonates were deposited in the form of limestones—over 10,000 feet of them. These limestones today form the floors of the Hagerstown and Frederick valleys.

Paleozoic Orogenies

Three different mountain-building episodes (orogenies) occurred about 450 to 250 mya (Middle Ordovician through Permian time). All three orogenies were part of the tectonic closing of the Iapetus Ocean. Two mountain ranges, the Taconic and the Acadian, were created by tectonic plate movements and then subjected to tens of millions of years of erosion and lowering before the final Alleghenian Orogeny, resulting from the collision of North America with Africa and Europe, produced the ancestors of the Appalachian Mountains (Figure 16-3).

During the Taconic Orogeny (440 to 420 mya in the central Appalachians) a land mass that had been carried on an oceanic plate through the ancient Iapetus Ocean collided with the continental edge of ancestral North America. The collision compressed and folded up into the Taconic Mountain range the existing rocks—the Catoctin volcanics and the overlying sandstones, shales and limestones. The deeper rocks, including the Catoctin and Weverton formations, at several thousand feet beneath the surface were subjected to greater heat and pressure than those lying nearer the surface.

Metamorphism resulted, changing the original volcanic basalt and rhyolite into the Catoctin metabasalt and metarhyolite, and the original sandstone into the Weverton quartzite. Millions of years later, during the Acadian Orogeny (about 360 mya), a similar sequence of land mass collision, mountain building and metamorphism occurred.

During and after these land-uplifting events, the weathering, transport and deposition of sediment were continuously occurring—particularly in seas that existed inland from the Taconic and Acadian mountain ranges. As the weather of hundreds of millions of years gradually lowered first the Taconics and then the Acadians, huge amounts of sediment were carried westward into inland seas that existed over western Pennsylvania, West Virginia, Ohio and other areas. Mixed intermittently with this inorganic material were thick layers of the remains of marine organisms. These thick wedges of deposits slowly compacted and cemented into sandstone, shale, and limestone rock at the bottom of the inland seas (Figure 17-3). Today these rocks comprise the mountains and hills of the Appalachian areas—raised into their upland positions by the final and most powerful orogeny, the Alleghenian, which was caused by the collision of North America, Africa and other continents.

The Alleghenian Orogeny resulted when all of the continents collided and formed the supercontinent Pangaea. This orogeny thus occurred when the ancient ocean closed between the southeastern edge of our continent and the northwestern edge of Africa. When the two gigantic plates shoved relentlessly into each other over the course of about 60 million years (about 325 mya to about 265 mya), the tectonic stress did more than just uplift the inland rock wedges (Figure 16-4).

The entire Blue Ridge-Piedmont, all along what is now the inland eastern United States, was detached as a massive block in a sheet from a layer deep within the earth and shoved 100 miles or more westward. The block, known as the Blue Ridge-Piedmont thrust sheet, drove the foreland into huge folds (wavelike structures of rock) that produced mountains perhaps 20,000 feet high. The thrust sheet also ramped itself up onto some of the existing sedimentary rocks and created numerous fractures and movements (faults) in these rocks.

Hagerstown Valley, for example, just west of the Blue Ridge, is a highly faulted terrane, as is the entire Great Valley that runs through Pennsylvania, Maryland and Virginia.

In the area of the Catoctins, geological evidence from the eastern slopes, and from South Mountain to the west, suggests that a large anticlinorium, a regional-sized upwarped arch of a mountain, once stretched from the area that is today the Frederick Valley to the area 10 to 15 miles west that is today the Hagerstown Valley (Figure 17-4). This anticlinorium was part of the thrust sheet; it was driven by the tremendous compressive force of tectonic collision into a huge fold or wave of rock, which was both over-turned and ramped or sheared up over younger limestone rocks that now lie in the Hagerstown Valley. This severe bending of rock layers into an arch-like structure probably occurred many hundreds of feet beneath the surface, where the increased heat and pressure would cause the rock to behave in a plastic or bendable manner.

The overlying rock, long since eroded, would likely have given the ancestral Catoctin Mountains a height of 15,000 to 20,000 feet. Over 200 million years of erosion have washed that material toward the ocean and other basins, thus removing the top of the anticlinorium and reducing the highest elevations to slightly less than 2,000 feet.

East of the Catoctins, in what is known as the Piedmont area, and even down to Baltimore, are the remnants of the terranes that were carried into North America by the plate movements associated with the Taconic and Acadian orogenies. Geologists call these suspect terranes—microplate fragments that accrete to the margin of a continent. Because they have been in place for over 200 million years, they are difficult to identify simply by looking at the landscape.

Triassic Downfaulting and Erosion

About 200 million years ago the supercontinent Pangaea began to break apart. As in Precambrian time, the ocean began to open—this time it was to become the Atlantic Ocean. As Africa and Europe moved away from North America, the compressive forces were released, and crustal extension caused large areas of rock to fracture and slide downward (Figure 16-5). One major vein of downfaulting occurred along a line from Nova Scotia to South Carolina, over millions of years, and resulted in huge troughs known as the Triassic basins.

Locally this Triassic Border Fault lies just east of Catoctin and Cunningham Falls parks; it runs roughly beneath Thurmont and Catoctin Furnace and roughly parallels the Frederick Valley along the base of the mountain (Figure 17-5).

East of this fault the land dropped well over a mile during the course of millions of years. Today, lying over a mile beneath the surface of Frederick Valley, are the sections of the Weverton and Harpers rock formations which had previously been continuous with the outcrops now visible on the eastern slopes of the Catoctins (Figure 17-6). Into the resulting freshwater lake basins, for the last 200 million years, have flowed the sand and clay sediments eroded by water from the nearby mountaintops. The Catoctins, if viewed from a few miles to the east, can be seen to protrude from the relatively flat area of this filled trough (Figure 18). The rock of the flat valley comprises sandstone and shale.

Mesozoic and Cenozoic Erosion

During the past 200 million years, the former 20,000 foot mountains were eroded to hills with elevations less than 2,000 feet. Most of the eroded material was deposited east of the Catoctins by streams carrying suspended and dissolved sediment and by mass wasting—downslope movement of rock material caused by gravity. Stream deposits are called alluvial, while mass wasting deposits are called colluvial. In these relatively young deposits can be found pieces of the older rock that eroded from mountaintops uplifted millions of years ago.

Mixed colluvial and alluvial deposits of Quaternary age—less than 3 million years old—underlie much of the Thurmont area, east of the parks. Much of this material was deposited by the ancestors of the present mountain creeks. Their sediment loads were kept in suspension during the rocky, turbulent descents of the eastern slopes of the Catoctin Mountains; this sediment fell out of the streams when their speed and turbulence suddenly decreased upon reaching the relatively flat terrain at the base of the mountain. Heavy deposits may have been made during Ice Age times, when the precursors of Hunting Creek and other streams may have carried larger volumes of water.

These Quaternary deposits lie all along the line marking the base of the Catoctins on the southeast but are thickest and widest where streams flow down and out from the mountains (Figure 14). The deposits consist of boulders, cobbles, pebbles and sand derived from the Weverton quartzite and the Catoctin metabasalt and metarhyolite.

Also present in the area are Quaternary alluvial deposits situated above the present flood plains of streams. A large portion of these silt and clay deposits may also be left over from the periglacial Ice Age times when the streams probably carried much more water.

Figure 16

Frames 1–6 cover almost one billion (1,000 million) years of the geologic history of eastern North America. The diagrams are idealized and very general, and the dates are approximate. Arrows indicate *relative* motion of crustal plates and pieces, which are represented as "floating" on the plastic, semi-molten asthenosphere.

1) Rifting and Spreading: 800–600 mya
Separation of crustal pieces creates an ancient ocean and micro-continents. On the North American plate—much smaller than it is today—crustal extension results in fractures and faults in the basement rock. The ancient, previously existing Grenville Mountains, formed over one billion years ago, lie to the west.

2) Subsidence and Deposition: 600–450 mya
The ocean widens and deepens as the plates continue to separate. The Grenville Mountains erode, and rivers and streams carry the sediment offshore, where a large wedge of deposits is laid down.

3) Taconic and Acadian Mountain Building: 450–350 mya
As plates converge, microcontinents and islands collide with North America to form mountains, and land mass is added to the plate. Two major mountain-building events occur (only one is illustrated here). In each case, sediments erode from the mountains and wash into inland sea bottoms.

4) Alleghenian Orogeny: 325–265 mya
The African plate collides with the North American plate. Rock in the inland basin is caught in the converging vise and is folded up into lofty mountains. Some rock layers are thrust up over others.

5) Spreading and Rifting: 225–200 mya
Once again the continents separate and an ocean is formed. On land the crustal extension again causes fractures and down-faulting of huge blocks.

6) Present-day Sea Floor Spreading and Continent-edge Deposition
North America and Africa continue their separation as the sea floor spreads apart near the middle of the Atlantic Ocean. With each passing year, these continents separate by an inch or two. Sediments eroded from the land are carried to the offshore ocean bottom.

Legend

C	Craton or tectonic block	**S**	Wedge of sediment deposited by erosion of land
A	Asthenosphere		
OC	Oceanic crust	**TF**	Thrust faults and folds due to collision of tectonic plates
SC	Spreading center (separating ocean crust)	**NF**	Normal (block) faults due to crustal extension

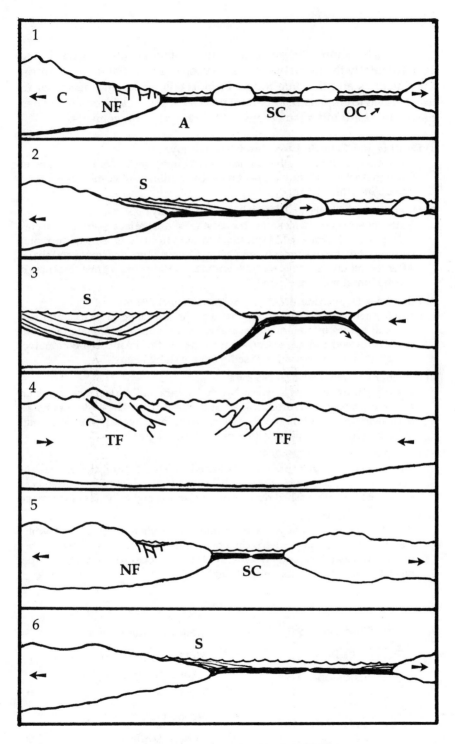

Figure 16. See text on page 26. Diagrams based on Hatcher, 1989.

27

Figure 17

Frames 1–6 show idealized enlargements of the events shown in Figure 16, particularly the formation and alteration of rocks that today comprise the Catoctins and the Blue Ridge. Proportions, scales and distances are exaggerated to emphasize important processes. The rock layers shown here have moved around often because of tectonic plate movements.

1) Faulting and Catoctin Lava Flows: 800–600 mya
Break-up of ancient North America causes huge volumes of lava to flow up through fractures in the basement rock. Over millions of years the lava flows pile up into thick layers.

2) Offshore Subsidence and Deposition: 650–450 mya
As the ancient ocean widens and the coast subsides, the lava plain sinks deeper. On top of it are deposited sands, silts and clays from the erosion of the mountains on land; these sediments compact and cement into sandstones and shales. After the mountains have worn down to a certain point, a great thickness of marine limestone is deposited.

3) Inland-sea Deposition: 450 mya onward, for over 100 my
The former offshore wedge now has a mountain range to its east and new material erodes into an inland sea. Tens of millions of years later a second range is formed and more deposits are added to this inland, sea-bottom rock wedge. (Not all of the layers of sediment are shown here.)

4) Alleghenian Orogeny: 325–265 mya
In the gigantic collision between North America and Africa, rock layers are metamorphosed, fractured, folded and overturned. High mountains are formed above the present-day landscape, represented by the dashed line. South Mountain Anticlinorium occupies most of the diagram.

5) Rifting and Faulting: 225–200 mya
As continents separate, pressure is released. The basement rock fractures and huge blocks slide down—creating basins and inland seas. Into these pour sediments that are washed down from the young and lofty mountain range.

6) Present-day Landscape
Over tens of millions of years, the mountains erode to form the hills which are present today. The eroded sediment has filled the basins and been washed toward the eastern shores. Present-day mountain tops are formed by the rock types that resisted erosion most strongly.

Legend

Basement rock		Metamorphosed lava	
Lava flow		Metamorphosed sandstone (quartzite)	
Sandstone			
Shale		**TF**	Thrust fault
Limestone		**NF**	Normal fault
Ocean or sea		**P**	Present landscape

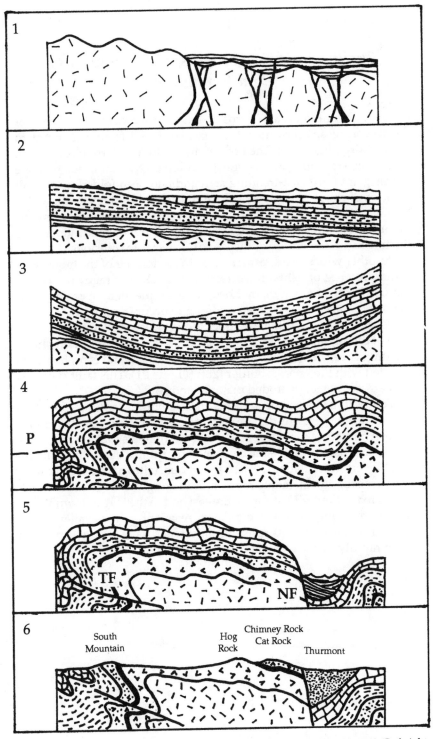

Figure 17. See text on page 28. Diagrams based on Cloos, 1947; Fauth, 1977, 1968; Gathright, 1976.

Visible Evidence of Crustal Compression and Extension

Over 200 million years of erosion have worn away the top layers of the towering anticlinorium that had stretched from Thurmont to Smithsburg (Figure 20). The beds of the Chilhowee Group (Loudoun, Weverton, Harpers) had previously underlain the southeastern slope of this giant northeast-trending arch and had been folded up to a tilt or slope of about 20 degrees. This southeasterly 20-degree dip, with a strike to the northeast, can be observed in some road cuts and mountaintop outcrops (Figure 13). It is both reminder and evidence of the force and magnitude of the Paleozoic tectonic collisions.

Another widespread result related to the folding of the mountains is the presence of joints (fractures) in the rock. The many joints that can be observed at Chimney Rock, for example, demonstrate conditions necessary for frost or ice wedging to occur (Figure 19).

A fault—a fracture in the bedrock along which movement of one or both of the adjoining rock masses has occurred—is present along Little Hunting Creek, just across from Catoctin Furnace, and is probably associated with the Triassic border fault (Figure 21). This fault is buried beneath many feet of eroded material and soil.

The tectonic collisions and the Triassic border fault are only two reasons for the present-day topographic relief of the Catoctin Mountains. Another is the widespread existence of rocks that are highly resistant to erosive forces—the hard, metamorphic rocks of the Catoctin and Weverton formations. These tough quartzites and metavolcanics have resisted the elements much more strongly than have the limestones in the Frederick Valley to the east and in the Hagerstown Valley to the west, and have come to form resistant ridges. Valleys were formed because the less resistant limestones have been worn down more rapidly by the elements.

Figure 18. The Triassic-age border fault is delineated where the relatively flat land meets the mountains. Geologic formations which at one time were continuous with those at the tops of the present mountain now lie thousands of feet beneath the flat area.

Figure 19. Gravity causes rock to fracture at Chimney Rock. Fractures in bedrock along which there is no movement of the adjacent rock masses are called joints.

31

W   E

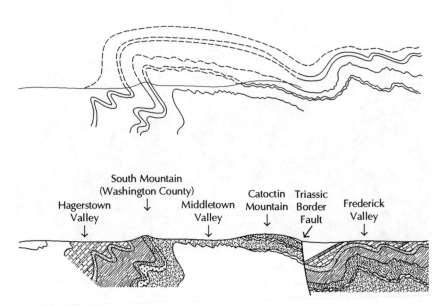

Figure 20. Top: The high, youthful mountains of Frederick and Washington counties, more than 200 mya. **Bottom:** The present geological cross-section of Hagerstown Valley, South Mountain, Middletown Valley, the Catoctins, and Frederick Valley. Note that the bedrock east of the fault has dropped so that geologic layers which were once mountaintops today lie far beneath Frederick Valley (after Cloos, 1958, and Cleaves, et al., 1968).

Pleistocene Periglacial Erosion

Freeze-and-Thaw near the Glacier

The Pleistocene Epoch, the most recent Ice Age, began over 2 million years ago and ended about 10,000 years ago. During this time up to about one-third of the earth's land surface was covered with ice. In the eastern United States the southernmost limit of the continental ice sheet, which approached from the north, was between Wilkes-Barre and Hazelton in northeastern Pennsylvania. The Catoctins were only about 100 miles from the edge of the ice-covered area.

Because of this proximity and because of their elevation, the Catoctins experienced a periglacial (near-glacial) environment. Conditions included discontinuous permafrost, tundra-like vegetation and, most importantly,

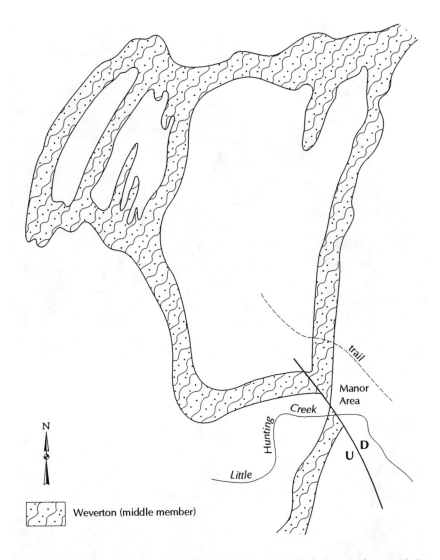

Figure 21. In this fault near the Manor Area of Cunningham Falls State Park, one side has been thrust upwards ("U")—creating displacement in the dipping middle member of the Weverton Formation. Evidence of the fault is hard to find because it has been largely covered by eroded material (from Fauth, 1977).

dozens of days per year of nighttime freeze and daytime thaw cycles—conditions that were most frequent during spring and fall.

Daytime thawing of snow and ice that lay on mountaintop rock outcrops allowed water to trickle into fractures in rock. During nights, when the water froze and expanded, it eventually wedged off thousands of boulders and smaller rocks, which fell into piles, known as talus, at the bases of outcrops (Figure 22 and 23). These fragments, in a process called solif-

Figure 22. This mountaintop outcrop near Chimney Rock displays many fractured rocks. Melting water fills spaces, freezes and expands, and breaks away pieces of rock in a process known as frost wedging.

Figure 23. This deposit, located below Chimney Rock, resembles a talus pile. If the area were subjected to periglacial conditions, downslope solifluction might occur.

Figure 24. Angular rocks in the foreground have been moved downslope by solifluction from the eroding outcrop in the background. Cracks indicate that freeze-and-thaw frost wedging continues in these rocks located just off of Crows Nest Trail.

luction, then crept downslope, as a slowly sliding layer of water-saturated rock and soil above a deeper, frozen layer of ground (Figure 24).

At the end of the Pleistocene the slopes of the Catoctins were left littered with stones. Valley bottoms collected many of the stones, and today water tumbles over these rock-strewn courses. Many mountain slopes have "stone streams" that run from the outcropping cliff at the mountaintop all the way down to the base of the slope (Figures 25 and 26).

The presence of the stone streams, or block fields, in the parks is evidence of Pleistocene solifluction. Subsequent erosion, mostly by water, has carried away the smaller material and left the larger stones. That the boulder fields are stable today is evidenced by the undisturbed presence of lichen on the top sides of the boulders and by the presence of mature trees that are unscarred and untilted (Figures 27 to 30).

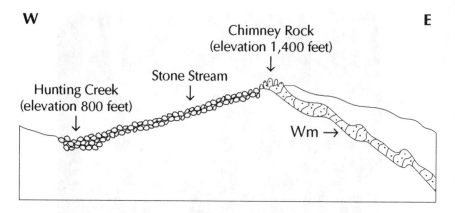

W

E

Chimney Rock
(elevation 1,400 feet)

Stone Stream

Hunting Creek
(elevation 800 feet)

Wm →

Figure 25. This generalized cross-section from Chimney Rock to the bend in the creek and road just below the Administrative Office shows the long stone stream that runs from Chimney Rock, an outcrop of the highly-resistant, ridge-forming middle member of the Weverton Formation (wm). The stone stream is believed to have developed during the most recent Ice Ages when the Catoctins, though not covered by the continental glacier, were subjected to frequent cycles of freeze-and-thaw erosion.

Figure 26. These huge boulders and deep crevasses at Chimney Rock mark the head of the stone stream that runs continuously downslope to Hunting Creek.

Figure 27. A side-slope stone stream. The angular shape of the rock and the size of several boulders are evidence of solifluction associated with the most recent Ice Age. Untilted trees indicate that this slope, which once experienced solifluction, is now stable.

Another convincing piece of evidence that the stone streams were ice-deposited is that the stones are angular, typical of frost-wedging, whereas rocks deposited by running water are usually rounded.

Since the Catoctins still have 50 to 100 freeze-and-thaw cycles per year, frost wedging can be observed on individual stones where a lichen-free, unweathered surface is visible.

Guide to Exploring Stone Streams

The stone streams of the Catoctins have been classified by geologists into three basic types. Some of them are visible from existing trails.

1) **Boulder-covered slopes** are areas covered by boulders that are up to 20 feet long and spaced less than 50 feet apart; the boulders are mostly of the Weverton Formation. Boulder-covered slopes lie adjacent to the trails to Cat Rock, Chimney Rock and Wolf Rock, and Bobs Hill to the south toward Little Hunting Creek Valley; and on the slope down to Owens Creek, north of the trail to Thurmont Vista.

2) **Side-slope stone streams** are linear deposits up to a half-mile long and 50–500 feet across, usually bordered at the head by scarps or outcrops of the Weverton Formation. These are made up of boulders

37

that average 3 feet in length and are spaced less than 2 feet apart. Some boulders may be up to 11 feet long (Figure 27).

The most accessible stone streams are below the Catoctin Park Administrative Office and "flow" into Hunting Creek. One is upslope from the 90-degree bend in the creek just below the office; it can be reached higher up by following the trail to Chimney Rock or the Crows Nest Trail (Figure 30). The other is about one-quarter mile below the office, just past the next 90-degree bend in the creek. It can be seen from the road just below where Bear Branch flows under the road (Figure 29).

Another lies just upstream from the parking lot across Route 77 from the Administrative Office. Follow the path by the creek a few feet upstream from the parking lot and look left, up the hill.

3) **Valley-bottom stone streams** are linear boulder deposits that occupy the stream bottoms. Almost anywhere along Hunting Creek, from Cunningham Falls to the park boundary, these valley deposits can be seen. The area from the falls to the lake affords what is probably the best view (Figure 28).

Figure 28. Below Cunningham Falls, Hunting Creek flows through a valley bottom filled with stones moved there by solifluction during the Ice Age.

Figure 29. A lengthy stone stream visible from Route 77, just below the mouth of Bear Branch at Hunting Creek—see Figure 30.

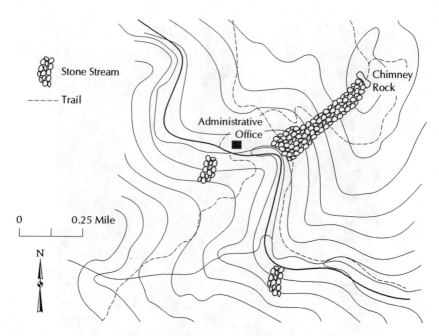

Figure 30. Two stone streams are located near the Catoctin Mountain Park Administrative Office and one near the mouth of Bear Branch. Note the parking areas and the pull-off near Bear Branch (After Godfrey, 1975).

Streams, Water Resources and Hydrology

Hydrology of the Catoctin Mountains

The three main streams that drain the Catoctins in the area of the two parks are Owens Creek, Big Hunting Creek and Little Hunting Creek. Each has its headwaters in the higher elevations of the Catoctin metavolcanic formations, and each flows eastward, emerging onto the Frederick Valley near the Triassic border fault (roughly along Route 15).

Every stream or river is surrounded by a particular land area that contributes water to it. This area, measured to the mouth of the stream—where it empties into a larger stream, river or body of water—is called the drainage basin, watershed or catchment. For example, Big Hunting Creek has a drainage area of 41.8 square miles and a length of about 15 miles from its highest point to its mouth at the Monocacy River. Owens Creek drains an area of 39.8 square miles.

A line that separates different basins along the highest elevations of ridges and hilltops is called a drainage divide (Figure 31). Part of the drainage divide between Owens and Hunting creeks runs roughly along Park Central Road from Round Meadow to the parking area for Thurmont Vista. Precipitation falling north of this ridge drains into Owens Creek; that falling south of it drains into a tributary of the main trunk of Big Hunting Creek (Figure 32).

The stream that generally forms the boundary between the national and the state parks is Big Hunting Creek. It flows over Cunningham Falls and fills Hunting Creek Lake. Since Big Hunting Creek is the most visible and most visited of the streams in the parks, it will be used as a reference throughout this section and will hereafter be called by its more common name "Hunting Creek."

Stream Gradient

The slope, or drop, of a stream determines the flow velocity. This measure of vertical drop over a certain horizontal distance is called **stream gradient**. A 6 percent slope or gradient, for example, means that a stream drops six feet vertically for every 100 feet that it flows horizontally. Hunting Creek has a relatively steep gradient in its mountain section—in the parks—but has a flatter slope and slower flow across the Frederick Valley to the Monocacy River. Ninety-five percent of its drop, from highest point to mouth, occurs above Bentz Pond, which is near the eastern park boundaries. A cross-section through the stream bed reveals the changing gradient of Hunting Creek (Figure 33).

Stream gradient varies according to terrain and geologic structure. The upper part, from a marshy area near the Route 77 and Stottlemeyer Road intersection, at an elevation of 1,450 feet, to the top of Cunningham Falls, at 1,300 feet, has a gradient of 2.2 percent over a length of 1.3 miles. This

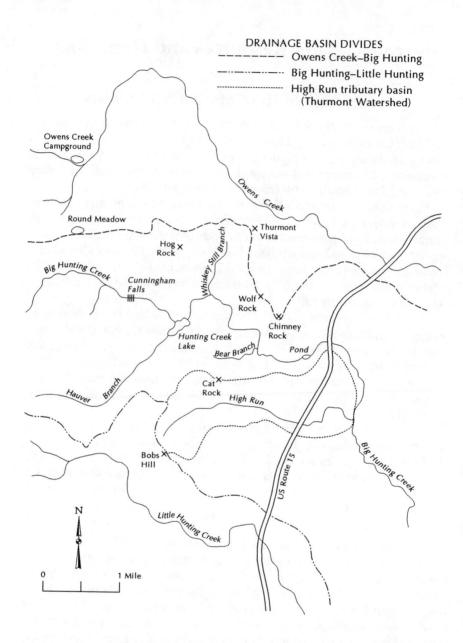

DRAINAGE BASIN DIVIDES
- - - - - - - Owens Creek–Big Hunting
- ·· - ·· - ·· - Big Hunting–Little Hunting
·················· High Run tributary basin
(Thurmont Watershed)

Owens Creek
Campground

Owens Creek

Round Meadow

Thurmont
Vista

Hog ✕
Rock

Whiskey Still Branch

Big Hunting Creek

Cunningham
Falls

Wolf ✕
Rock

Chimney
Rock

Hunting Creek
Lake

Bear Branch

Pond

Hauver Branch

Cat ✕
Rock

High Run

Big Hunting Creek

Bobs ✕
Hill

US Route 15

N

0   1 Mile

Little Hunting Creek

Figure 31. The streams of the Catoctins run generally from west to east. They run through valleys and the highest points on the ridges that separate the valleys form a line that is known as a drainage divide. Drainage divides for the principal streams of the parks are shown here. Note that High Run is a tributary of Big Hunting Creek. Most of its drainage basin is not part of the parks' acreage but comprises the Thurmont city watershed. Watershed is another word for drainage basin.

Figure 32. This view looks north across the valley of Hunting Creek from Cat Rock. Precipitation falling on the slopes facing Cat Rock drains into Hunting Creek. Precipitation on the opposite, non-visible slope drains into Owens Creek.

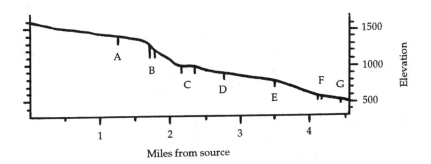

Figure 33. Stream profile of Hunting Creek from its source at 1,600-foot elevation southwest of Foxville to the Route 15 interchange west of Thurmont: A, park boundary on Route 77; B, Cunningham Falls; C, Hunting Creek Lake; D, Visitor Center; E, bend in creek and road below Administrative Office; F, Bentz Pond; G, Route 15.

Figure 34. Near its headwaters in the western half of Catoctin Park, on the metarhyolite, Owens Creek has a gentle slope.

gradient is similar to that of Owens Creek in its upper reaches, as shown in Figure 34.

From the top of the Falls to the beach at the state park, where it enters the lake at an elevation of 1,000 feet, Hunting Creek has a steep gradient of 9.4 percent over 0.6 mile. Here it flows over a valley bottom stone stream, as shown in Figure 35.

From below the dam at an elevation of 920 feet, down past the Visitor Center to the Administrative Office at 800 feet, Hunting Creek covers 1.3 miles with a mild 1.8 percent gradient.

From the Catoctin Park Administrative Office down to Frank Bentz Pond just outside the park boundary, at 590 feet, the gradient again becomes steeper at 3.6 percent over 1.1 miles (Figure 36).

The changes in slope along Route 77 roughly parallel those of Hunting Creek.

Water Flow Within a Drainage Basin

Precipitation makes its way from hillslope to stream along three different paths (Figure 37):

1) **overland flow**—If the ground is hard-packed, frozen or already saturated with water, additional water cannot infiltrate, and it drains over the top of the land, usually eroding soil with it.

2) **subsurface flow**—Water can drain downslope within the soil if the soil thickness above bedrock is deep and permeable, if hillslopes are steep, and if vegetation is dense. These conditions allow precipitation to infil-

Figure 35. Below Cunningham Falls, Hunting Creek tumbles over a valley bottom strewn with rocks and boulders left by periglacial Ice Age erosion.

trate the soil more easily and to flow downslope through small, subsurface openings in the soil instead of on top of the land.

3) **groundwater base flow**—Water moves at a slow, steady rate, many feet below the surface, through the zone of saturation (the "filled" area reaching up to the water table). Thick, permeable soil and vegetation allow water to soak in and percolate down into the groundwater.

For Hunting Creek, there is usually very little overland flow, unless the ground is saturated. Subsurface flow is an important source, contributing 30-40 percent of streamflow, because most of the hillside soil is a thick, permeable, stony loam, because hillsides are steep, and because vegetation is thick. About 55 percent of stream flow comes from groundwater that works its way down from high ground to the line where the groundwater intersects the stream bank—the surface of the stream. Here, beneath

Figure 36. The steep gradient of lower Hunting Creek and the rocky valley bottom result in beautiful falls and pools.

the surface, groundwater slowly but continuously flows into the stream. During periods of drought or little rain, this groundwater recharge maintains stream flow.

Periglacial erosion was partly responsible for the deep cover of sandy soil and loose stone over bedrock. Such cover means that water infiltrates and percolates downward quickly, a condition that explains why subsurface and groundwater base flow contribute nearly all of the water to the stream.

The Aquifer

An aquifer is a rock and soil layer that holds and transmits groundwater. In the Catoctin Mountains, a thick layer of very stony soil lies on top of the bedrock. Many feet below the surface, groundwater occupies the spaces between the soil and stone particles. Beneath the layer of stony soil in the bedrock, ground water is present in cracks and openings that have been enlarged by groundwater weathering. The number and size of the openings determines the porosity; the degree to which the openings are interconnected determines the permeability of the bedrock. The metabasalt, metarhyolite and quartzite bedrocks of the Catoctin Mountains have low porosity and low permeability—meaning that they transmit groundwater very slowly.

When rain water falls it percolates down through the soil and recharges the ground water. The upper surface of the subterranean saturated zone, known as the water table, rises and falls depending on the amount of pre-

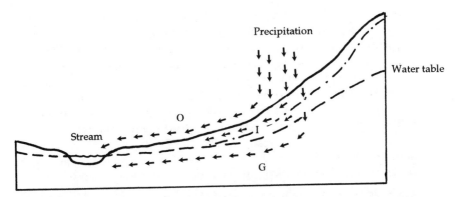

Figure 37. Possible routes by which water can move from a hillslope down to a stream or lake: O, overland flow; I, interflow or subsurface flow; G, groundwater base flow. Overland flow is the fastest; groundwater flow, the slowest. (After Dunne and Leopold, 1978.)

cipitation and on the amount of water used by vegetation. At springs and streams, as mentioned above, the water table intersects the surface. In other places, however, the water table lies tens of feet below the surface; there it can be tapped by wells, several of which are in the park.

Stream Flow and Sediment Load

The average discharge, or water-volume flow rate, of Hunting Creek is 3 to 5 cubic feet per second (22 to 38 gallons per second). The current, or stream velocity, varies according to the shape of the stream bed, the stream width and the gradient.

Stream velocity is fastest near the middle; it is slower on the sides and bottom, due to friction from the banks and stream bed. These ongoing differences in velocity create little eddies or whirlpools that pick up dirt from the stream bottom and sides. As long as water turbulence is sufficient, this suspended material, called the sediment load, is carried along. If velocity and turbulence decrease, as in a calm or quiet stretch, gravity takes over and some of the sediment load is dropped out of suspension and deposited back on the stream bed.

Streams and rivers continuously carry material from higher elevations down to lower elevations. The lowering of the Appalachians over millions of years was probably accomplished mostly by running water. The land that is now southern Maryland and the western shore of the Chesapeake Bay, as well as the land of the Delmarva Peninsula, have all been deposited since the creation of the Appalachians. Material from the mountains was thus carried by streams like Hunting Creek down to larger rivers for eventual deposit and the building up of new land.

Stream Location and Geology

When a land area is uplifted, as the Catoctins were over 200 million years ago, streams begin the process of downcutting or deepening valleys. As mass wasting and erosion from overland flow remove rock and soil from valley walls, a characteristic V-shaped valley forms. As with most forces in nature, a downcutting stream takes the course of least resistance: given the choice of cutting its channel into highly resistant rock or into moderately resistant rock, it will cut more rapidly into the less resistant rock to begin forming its channel.

The following three terrain features of Hunting Creek reveal much about the relationship between geologic structure and the water that flows over it. Each description is theoretical and highly simplified.

1) The location of two tributaries of Hunting Creek:
   a. the creek running down by Camp Misty Mount and Blue Blazes Whiskey Still;
   b. Hauver Branch, which parallels Catoctin Hollow Road and empties into the lake, where it joins Hunting Creek.

About 200 million years ago, as the tops of the high mountains began to erode, various streams cut down through several rock layers. These streams were on the cutting edge of the erosive processes that would remove several of these rock layers in their entirety.

At a relatively late stage in the mountain-lowering process, the Whiskey Still Creek and Hauver Branch may have established their modern channels by downcutting into the moderately-resistant Loudoun Formation of conglomerate and phyllite, since it was flanked on either side by highly resistant formations, the Catoctin and the Weverton (see the geologic map, Figure 14). Although these tributaries do not flow in the Loudoun Formation today, the structural orientation (dip and strike) of these rocks indicates that the less resistant Loudoun may have been the formation of choice for the initial downcutting trend that finally established the tributary valleys of what is today called Catoctin Hollow.

2) The water gap through the hard Weverton Formation just below the Catoctin Park Administrative Office.

Below the office at the bend in the road, Hunting Creek seems to defy nature by taking the course of *most* resistance: it cuts directly across and through one of the most resistant rock formations in the park: the Weverton quartzite. The explanation for such a water gap begins with a time when the ancestor of Hunting Creek flowed at a higher elevation, far above the Weverton.

At the time of the Triassic border fault along the eastern edge of the parks, the mountains would not only have been higher, but they would have been covered with thousands more feet of rock layers, which have since eroded. Into the fault basin to the east would have plunged streams from the high mountains. One of the largest was probably the precursor of Hunting Creek. As the mountains were being lowered through millions of years of erosion, Hunting Creek would have established its easterly flow on the rock layers that once lay above the Weverton. When its downcutting action finally encountered the edge of the highly resistant quartzites, stream direction was already well-established at the bottom of a V-shaped valley, so the downcutting continued, eventually carving the water gap in the Weverton ridge below the Administrative Office (see Figure 12). A gap formed in a similar way—but on a much larger scale—may be seen where the Potomac River cuts through the Weverton Formation and South Mountain at Weverton, Maryland.

At a relatively late stage geologically, the side slope stone stream from Chimney Rock would have slowly flowed into the Hunting Creek gap. These stones probably had a damming effect, resulting in the flood plain deposits on which Camp Peniel—now the Administrative Office—was built and creating the cascades below Peniel with a kind of spillway effect (see Figure 36).

3) The location of Cunningham Falls

About 1½ miles upstream from the Administrative Office, the area that today is Cunningham Falls would have been covered, after the uplift of the mountains, with several tilted or dipping formations, including the Loudoun and the Weverton. Today, of course, those layers have long eroded, leaving the Catoctin metavolcanics, but Hunting Creek would have cut its valley through the Loudoun and the Weverton before it began cutting into the Catoctin Formation of greenstone.

Something slowed the downcutting, though, and produced a falls rather than a downsloping V-shaped valley of fairly constant gradient. There are at least two possible explanations, and perhaps each is correct:

1. Cunningham Falls might occur where the downcutting stream encountered the thickest and most resistant central sections of the ancient Precambrian lava flow.

2. Over a thousand feet beneath the greenstone of the falls area might lie an even more ancient, buried hill of granite. Remember that many parts of the ancient Grenville Mountains of granite were covered by the massive lava flow that today is the Catoctin Formation.

In either case, the downcutting stream encountered a formation through which it could not downcut at a constant rate. In former times, the falls were undoubtedly located downstream, for all waterfalls cut their ways upstream. One look at Cunningham Falls today verifies that this process is continuing (Figures 38 and 39).

Figure 38. Cunningham Falls flows over the metabasalt, or greenstone, a thick rock layer resulting from an ancient lava flow. Notice how the stream continues to cut into the rock.

Figure 39. Cunningham Falls, with water frozen.

Erosion and Deposition

Erosion, by definition, is the removal and transport of material. The eroded pieces may range in size from a large stone to a minute speck of clay. Formation of stream sediment load, a natural process, is an example of erosion.

When a stream makes a turn, the section of fastest flow is shifted from the middle of the stream toward the outside of the bend. The water flows into the outside bank and removes pieces of it, as the bank turns the flow downstream. The result is gradual undercutting and washout of the bank, or bank erosion. Most erosion occurs during high water, when forces are multiplied, and huge gouges may be cut, undermining streamside trees and causing them to fall across the stream (Figure 40).

Before erosion control devices were erected on some banks of Hunting Creek, this phenomenon could be observed on the outsides of bends at several locations. The first bend downstream from Catoctin Hollow Road exhibited this erosion. Also, the stream bank closest to the visitor center was once undercut because it is on the outside of a long, sweeping stream bend (Figure 41). A structure called cribbing has since been installed to shore up the bank and help control future erosion (Figure 42).

While the stream velocity is fastest near the outside portions of a bend, it is slowest near the inside. Here the turbulence decreases, and the water becomes relatively calm. Some of the sediment load will fall out of suspension to the stream bottom because there is no longer sufficient water activity and energy to carry the particles along in the current.

Figure 40. Not far downstream from where Hunting Creek flows under Catoctin Hollow Road, high water has worked to undercut these trees on the outside of a bend.

Figure 41. Across the road from Catoctin Park Visitor Center (about 1989–1990) Hunting Creek has eroded the bank, causing the collapse and felling of a large tree into the stream. Note that the eroded bank is on the outside of a long, sweeping bend.

The inside of a stream bend is called the depositional side because particles of the sediment load, carried down from upstream, are dropped (deposited) there. After periods of high water a depositional area can be expanded, and large deposits of sand and gravel can be left behind when flood waters recede. Thus particles of the channel or bank on the outer, erosional side of a bend are removed and transported downstream, where they might be deposited at the inside of another bend (Figure 43).

The Dam

The artificial lake at Cunningham Falls State Park is created by an earthen dam across Hunting Creek. The lake covers about 43 acres and impounds about 250 million gallons of water. Its primary purpose is recre-

Figure 42. A completed cribbing structure, just upstream from the site shown in Figure 41. Although the structures are not visually pleasing to all fishermen, their presence helps to absorb the erosive energy of the stream flow and to keep trees on the bank—which means shade for the water and cooler temperatures for the fish.

Figure 43. As Hunting Creek bends to the right (flowing away from the foreground), the bank and the tree root systems on the erosional side are undermined. On the depositional side, sand and rocks are laid down in a flat, beach-like deposit.

Figure 44. The lake and dam during winter.

Figure 45. The lake and dam during summer.

ation: swimming, boating and fishing. Because of the lake's recreational purpose, the water level is not significantly lowered prior to the rainy season; therefore, the dam has only a limited flood control function (Figures 44 and 45).

However, the dam is beneficial to Hunting Creek trout stream, which runs below it, in three ways:

1) As a sediment trap: When any turbid, muddy flow from the headwaters enters the reservoir, the sudden drop in flow rate and turbulence causes sediment to fall out to the lake bottom. Therefore, water emerging below the dam is clear and cleansed of sediment.

2) As a flow control: A low flow of 1.5 cubic feet per second is guaranteed by the State Park. This rate approaches the base flow of Hunting Creek—the amount that groundwater alone contributes. Although this does not seem to be much of a flow, during dry summers it has been enough to prevent trout tail fins from being exposed in the creek below. In other words, without the dam the groundwater discharge during drought periods might not be sufficient to provide enough water for the trout to live.

3) As a temperature control: By drawing from three ports at three lower levels, the dam discharges cold water, which is helpful to the trout during a hot summer. The temperature of a trout stream should not exceed 65°F, but in the hot summer of 1988, it was measured in the 67°–73°F range. It might have been higher were it not for the dam.

Basic Ingredients for a Trout Stream

Hunting Creek is probably the most heavily fished trout stream in Maryland, although only fly fishing and catch-and-return are allowed. Such a good trout stream requires specific conditions, which can be endangered by natural events, as well as by man's presence. However, man can do much to enhance natural stream conditions and to protect the stream from the hazards of civilization. Each category of conditions requires attention.

1. Water

In order to sustain a healthy variety of aquatic organisms, the stream should have sufficient quantity and quality of water for every day of the year. For Hunting Creek, the dam is beneficial because it guarantees a baseflow of 1.5 cubic feet per second and because it acts as a sediment trap to reduce turbidity (muddiness). In addition, because most of the drainage basin is government owned, the stream can be protected against most sources of pollution.

2. Temperature

Trout stream temperature should not exceed 65°F. During summer, water is discharged from the cold depths of the lake above the dam to help keep stream temperature down.

The best protection against temperature increase is streamside trees, which provide shade. Often, however, bank erosion and undercutting cause trees to fall into the stream and leave the stream exposed to the warming rays of the sun. Devices such as deflectors and sills can help prevent bank erosion by controlling the direction of stream flow.

These devices can also reduce the area of stream surface by narrowing the channel. With less water surface exposed to the summer air and the sun, the stream will remain cooler.

3. Food

Trout prefer to eat aquatic insects, which thrive in a shallow, well-aerated area that is free of silt. These qualities are found in sections of fast-moving water called riffles. These are the areas of primary food production, including not only insect larvae but the periphyton (diatoms, algae, water moss) on which insect larvae feed. Periphyton, being at the bottom of the food chain in a stream, are so important that the general health of a stream can be measured by sampling and determining periphyton diversity.

Riffle wave action and fast water flow wash clear any silt that might deposit a choking cover; the cleared-out areas between creek stones provide protected crannies for aquatic insect larvae. The riffle action also provides good air-water interaction, which increases the amount of dissolved oxygen in the water. Streamside trees again are important because detritus (leaf litter) is a base for much of this food production.

Changes in the ecosystem, such as a reduction in oxygen, an increase in temperature or an increase in pollutants, can cause a decrease in periphyton diversity, aquatic insect production and trout population.

4. Shelter and Cover

Pools are necessary because the shy trout seek shelter and coolness in deep water and beneath undercut banks, overhanging vegetation, rocks and logs. A stream that is too wide, too shallow or all riffles is not a good trout habitat.

Pools are also necessary because they are sites of decomposition. In the slower current, the organic materials settle out and begin decomposing. This process generates carbon dioxide, which also is associated with an increase in pH (an increase in alkalinity), a condition necessary for increased aquatic life and trout population. The acidic precipitation that now falls on the park threatens to destroy this productive process. (See *Acid Rain* in the **Environmental Problems** section below.)

The best proportion of pools and riffles is about 1:1. On the flatter portions of Hunting Creek, the addition of jack dams and deflectors has created new pools and riffles, where wide, shallow conditions existed previously, in an effort to achieve the 1:1 proportion (Figures 46 and 47).

These structures can be observed in the sections above and below the mouth of Bear Branch, about 1½ miles down Route 77 east of the visitor center.

Good stream management usually begins on the banks. Activities such as heavy foot traffic or construction can damage tree growth and contribute to increased siltation of the stream.

Figure 46. Upstream from the bend below the mouth of Bear Branch, this series of log dams creates a pool-and-riffle habitat where the stream would otherwise flow straight and unmixed over this relatively flat stretch.

Figure 47. Downstream from the reference point of Figure 46 is a section of natural pools and riffles. The trees, in excellent condition here, enhance and protect stream habitat by trapping eroding soil from adjacent land, holding soil in place with their root structure, providing shade to maintain cool water temperature, providing cover for fish and contributing detritus to the food chain.

5. Reproduction

The trout nest (redd), where the eggs are laid, must be a gravelly area free of silt. It must remain silt-free while the eggs incubate and hatch, and until the fry are able to swim freely.

Sections of riffle are necessary because well-aerated water must pass through the redd continuously to provide oxygen and to carry away waste products given off by eggs and fry. Areas of hydraulic upwelling are favorite spots for trout spawning.

Stream structures that narrow the stream and speed up flow create the clean, gravelly bottom necessary for both trout spawning and aquatic insect production.

Disaster can occur if a large amount of dirt is suddenly washed into a stream. As it settles on the bottom, it clogs the spaces between the gravel and covers the redd. Without sufficient oxygen from the water, the eggs die. Aquatic insects, aquatic plants and adult fish can also be smothered in this way.

In the two parks, protection against siltation is afforded by the dam; two other preventative measures are maintenance of vegetation throughout the drainage basin and prevention of stream bank erosion wherever possible.

Stream and Streambank Structures

During the 1980s and early 1990s the Stream Committee of C.A.M.P.E.R., a previously existing volunteer group, constructed several stream and bank devices on Hunting Creek. Designed to control bank erosion and enhance trout habitat, the installed devices include single and double log frame deflectors, jack or log dams, and other bank stabilization structures. These devices can be observed on Hunting Creek in the grassy area across Route 77 from the Visitor Center or in the long, straight section after the 90° bend that is below the Catoctin Park Administration Office.

The following charts give information on the design and function of these streambank structures.

Low Flow Channel Structure: Jack Dam or Log Dam

Description	A log is placed across the stream to form a dam with a water drop of 12–16 inches. Wing deflectors may be used to prevent bank erosion.
Purpose	The purpose is not so much to create an upstream pool as it is to form a drop so that the falling water will dig a hole below the dam.
Effect on trout habitat	The pool of still water above the dam is a less suitable habitat because:

        · slower flow causes siltation of the bottom, and
        · warming of water can occur.

The water drop aerates the stream. An overhead cover is provided below the dam by the hole and by the dam structure. A scoured area with potential for spawning is generated below the dam (Figure 48).

Figure 48. The log dam helps to aerate the water and to scour an area below the dam for potential spawning.

Figure 49. Here a V-shaped log dam is combined with a double-winged deflector. The restriction in stream width increases flow rate for added aeration and scouring. The deflectors protect the banks and streamside trees from erosion.

Design and construction	The dam is located where the stream gradient is steep enough to minimize the size of the pool that is created. At least 18 inches of bank is required above the dam to prevent flooding. The dam is low (12–16 inches) so that fish can move up or down.
	Wing-walls (deflectors) above and below the dam prevent bank washout above and bank undercutting below (Figure 49). Wood stays wet all the time to prevent rot.
Example	The series of log dams below the Administrative Office creates alternate pools and riffles in a relatively flat, straight section that would naturally have very few pools or riffles (Figure 46).

Log Frame Deflector: Single and Double

Description	A triangular, rock-filled structure is anchored to the bank and protrudes only a few inches above normal stream flow.
Purpose	Single: Changes direction of stream flow to protect an eroding stream bank (Figure 50).
	Double: Speeds up stream flow. Narrows and deepens stream channel (Figure 49).
Effect on habitat	Single: Bank stabilization has several benefits:
	· Soil erosion and stream siltation are decreased.
	· Growth of streamside vegetation is enhanced.
	· Vegetation provides cover for fish.
	· Leaf litter adds to the food chain.
	· Shade lowers water temperature.
	Double: Faster flow has two benefits:
	· Silt is scoured to create gravelly crannies for improved aquatic insect and trout population.
	· Dissolved oxygen is increased in riffles.
Design and construction	Both types are log-framed and filled with hand-placed stone; they taper toward upstream bank at 30° angle:
	· a steeper angle would endanger the opposite bank with too much flow deflection;
	· a steeper angle would subject the deflector to too much force and increase the danger of damage.
	The logs extend 6 feet into the bank and are anchored with reinforcing bars 3 to 4 feet long.
Examples	Various types of deflectors can be seen in the grassy area across Route 77 from the Visitor Center.

Figure 50. Two single-wing deflectors prevent the current from continuing to undercut this bank on the outside of a bend.

Figure 51. Rock-filled cribbing on the erosional side not only prevents erosion but also shores up the badly scoured stream bank so that streamside trees can be saved.

Open Face Log Cribbing

Description A rectangular framework of logs, often with flooring, is filled with large rock on the bank of the stream.

Purpose Placed on an eroding or undercut stream bank, this device absorbs the impact of the stream current and provides a solid foundation for the bank.

Effect on habitat Because the stream is confined within its natural channel, it scours enough depth to handle normal water volumes. Shelter is provided for fish when the area under the structure is scoured.

Example One of these can be seen across Route 77 from the Visitor Center (Figure 51).

Stone Riprap

Description The riprap, a layer of stone that substitutes for natural soil and rock on the banks of a stream, approximates the natural slope of the bank.

Purpose The structure prevents bank washout during high water; absorbs stream energy and decreases velocity; protects structures such as roadbeds or bridges that may be threatened by water.

Effect on habitat Because the riprap may be above stream level, it has little direct effect, but it can help prevent siltation during a flood.

Design and construction Larger rocks are placed on lower levels, and the stone layer is usually about two feet thick. Hand placement is usually needed for proper distribution and attractive appearance.

Example The bridge on Catoctin Hollow Road over Hunting Creek has a riprap on each side (Figure 52).

Figure 52. A limestone riprap, made from rock hauled up from the valleys and not from the nearby mountains, protects the road and bridge from high water. Even though this bridge on Catoctin Hollow Road is below the dam, it has been known to be under water after heavy rains. The riprap here helps prevent washout of the roadbed, as is evidenced by pieces of limestone to be found hundreds of feet downstream from the bridge.

Forests

The Forests of the Catoctin Mountains

In 1936, when the National Park Service acquired over 10,000 acres of mountain land, the forest was exhausted following two hundred years of exploitation and abuse. Frank Mentzer, superintendent of Catoctin Park in the early 1970s, said, "In 1936 there was barely a tree over the size of a fence post."

The mountains had been interlaced with logging roads—Park Central Road follows what was probably an old logging road—and the forest resources had been devastated. For about 125 years the Catoctin Furnace iron industry required huge numbers of trees for its charcoal-fired furnaces. Many of the trees not used for charcoal were cut for sawmills or had their bark stripped for leather tanning operations.

Not all of the forest depletion was confined to the 19th century. In 1920, for example, over 5 million cubic feet of timber was cut. Over 500 men were employed in a wood industry, with almost 50 sawmills, to produce trolley and railroad ties, poles, staves, pulpwood, shingles, lath and cordwood (Figure 53).

Figure 53. The trees of the Catoctin Mountains in the 1920s (from Besley, 1922).

During the Depression of the 1930s, a new concept emerged: government-maintained recreational lands for the people. Forest regeneration was part of the federal government's plan to save non-productive land. The area that now makes up the two parks was originally known as the Catoctin Recreation Demonstration Area.

Succession and Climax Forest

For the Appalachians in general, the oak-hickory and, formerly, oak-chestnut associations of the eastern hardwood forest were the original, natural *climax forests*—the final, self-maintaining, stable plant communities of high species diversity that covers an area if left to develop without human or natural interference. After 200 years of human interference, however, some areas in the Catoctin Mountains may require almost that long to move from their disturbed condition through natural regeneration and back to climax vegetation (Figure 54).

Figure 54. The forest of the Catoctin Mountains is well on its way to climax after nearly sixty years of protection and management. Note the lush understory in this section near Owens Creek.

After clear cutting, regeneration of some of the existing climax tree species occurs through stump sprouting. In other areas, abandoned farm land or fields regenerate more slowly toward the climax forest in a process known as *secondary succession*: a series of ecological changes in which certain species of vegetation create an environment or conditions that cause them to be replaced gradually by other species, and those in turn by others, in a progressive sequence until the environment is right for the climax or "final" vegetation. Once established and mature, the different climax tree species continue to maintain and reproduce themselves without giving way to other species, unless there is another disturbance.

An old field, such as the one that was abandoned in the 1930s in what is now the Brown's Farm Environmental Study Area of Catoctin Park, provides a good example of secondary or "old field" succession. Because old field succession can take 100 to 150 years, parts of the Brown's Farm Area are only about halfway through the time frame needed for undisturbed progression to climax (Figure 55).

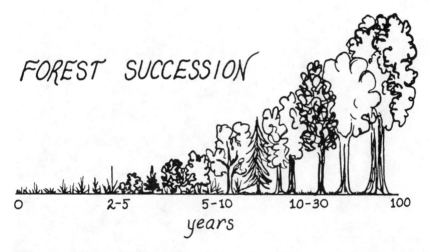

Figure 55. During old field succession the species composition goes through decades of change before the final, climax forest takes hold (from Brown's Farm Environmental Area trail guide).

The progressive stages of this century-long succession are (1) abandoned bare field, (2) weeds, (3) grassland, (4) grass-shrub-sapling, (5) intermediate forest and (6) climax forest. A brief history of the Brown's abandoned field might read as follows:

1) Hardy, resilient "weeds" with a high reproductive capacity (such as dandelion, thistle, crabgrass) invade the bare soil during the first year or two.

2) Perennial weeds and grasses move in during the next few years.

3) Shrubs (such as blackberry, raspberry, hawthorn) gradually appear and, with the grasses, hold moisture and provide shade for pioneer trees to take root. This grass-shrub phase lasts about 20 years.

4) Pioneer trees that are tolerant of the sun, such as black locust and tulip poplar, begin to grow, and the intermediate forest develops. Much of

the Brown's old field seems to be in this stage now—a stage that can last over 50 years (Figure 56). Note: The pine trees in this area were planted in the 1930s to control soil erosion and to provide food and cover for wildlife. Pines are not normally a part of the succession for this area.

5) As the intermediate forest develops, the earlier invaders—the grasses and shrubs—are shaded and gradually disappear. Into this shade are brought seeds of oak, hickory, beech, birch and maple by squirrels, birds, wind and other agents. The light, soil and moisture conditions are now right for the growth of these climax species.

Figure 56. In the Brown's Farm Area, where a barn once stood, pioneer species of trees have grown in the intermediate forest.

In some parts of the Brown's Farm Area, the intermediate forest is gradually yielding to the climax. Eventually the pioneer species will be out-competed by the climax species and the pioneers, too, will disappear.

The key to this natural development is for the species of each stage to generate gradually the conditions necessary for the next—conditions that ultimately lead to their own "sacrificial" disappearance to make room for the next, "higher" species.

In the Catoctins, succession has been well on its way since the mid-1930s, and in many areas the climax forest that the Indians and early colonists knew has been nearly restored (Figure 57). The virgin timber of those days has long since disappeared, but sound management and protection have restored the Mid-latitude Deciduous Forest on the bleak landscape that existed in the early 20th century. This type of forest is relatively rare on earth in that it turns into beautiful colors and sheds its leaves in fall, then bursts forth with new growth in spring.

Conditions Influencing the Types of Forest

Most of the parks' area contains a mixture of oaks, hickories, and tulip poplar that grow on generally rich soil. In a given area, however, the type of vegetation or forest community depends on many conditions: type of underlying bedrock, soil nutrients and moisture-holding capacity, hillslope steepness and aspect (the direction in which a slope is facing), elevation, average temperature and annual rainfall, previous human use, fires and invading organisms. Many of these conditions are interdependent, but perhaps the most influential is geology. Rock type and structure determine soil type, topography and elevation; they influence temperature, rainfall variation, and human activity.

Underlying Geologic Structure

The steeply dipping beds of the highly resistant Weverton quartzite in the eastern half of each park are responsible for narrow ridges and steep slopes, which have dry, acidic soils. In the western portions, the Catoctin metavolcanics form steep slopes and broad, flatter uplands, which have thick soils and good moisture retention (Figure 58). Along the creeks are flat, geologically-recent flood plain deposits that retain moisture well.

Soil Moisture and Nutrients

The soils in the eastern portions, those formed by the erosion of the Weverton quartzite, are thin, sandy loams. Water soaks into and through them very quickly; that is, they are highly permeable and well-drained. The ridge tops are the driest due to downslope drainage; trees which do not tolerate abundant moisture dominate here—chestnut oak and pitch pine. On the lower slopes and in ravines, where moisture is more abundant and soils deeper, grow sour gum, white oak, tulip poplar, red maple, black birch and eastern hemlock.

To the west the soils derived from metavolcanic rock are generally deeper, more moist and richer in nutrients (Figure 14). Generally the trees here are larger and the forests have a wider variety of species than those to the east. For example, near Hog Rock, an outcrop of the Catoctin metabasalt, a large moist area contains sugar maple, basswood, hickories, hornbeam, white ash, beech, tulip poplar and many others. An interpretive flyer for Hog Rock Nature Trail describes these species.

Figure 57. The climax forest of oak, hickory and beech near Chestnut Picnic Area. Notice the deer-browse line, where deer have removed all foliage as high as they could reach.

Figure 58. Hog Rock, visible in the foreground, and the woods below it are in the Catoctin metabasalt formation. The ridges to the east are topped by the Weverton quartzite.

While the drier ridge tops in the western portions are dominated by chestnut oak, moist areas on the flood plains near creeks contain trees that do not grow in drier areas: these include elm, river birch and sycamore.

Elevation, Temperature and Rainfall

Elevation is determined by the structure and resistivity of the underlying bedrock. Relief in and around the parks is quite varied. Nearby Thurmont is about 500 feet above sea level, and the Catoctin Mountain Park Visitor Center is at 920 feet. In the Weverton Formation, Wolf Rock and Chimney Rock are about 1,400 feet, Cat Rock 1,500 feet, and Bobs Hill 1,765 feet. In the Catoctin Formation, Hog Rock is at 1,620 feet, Chestnut Picnic Area 1,700 feet, the bottom of Cunningham Falls 1,300 feet, Hunting Creek Lake 988 feet—and the highest point of the parks, 1,880 feet.

Temperature and rainfall would be expected to be fairly consistent across the relatively small area of the Catoctins. However, variations might be expected because of topographic differences. Because most weather systems approach on the prevailing westerlies, slightly more rain might be expected on the windward or westerly-facing slopes.

Temperature varies dramatically with elevation. For every 1,000-foot rise in elevation, the average temperature drop is 3.5 degrees F. Put another way, every 100-foot rise in elevation is equivalent to travelling 20 to 25 miles northward.

Slope Angle and Aspect

In our northern latitude, the sun always travels across the southern portion of the sky—higher in summer, lower in winter. Because of this southern lighting, slopes that are facing toward the south are warmer than those in the shade of north-facing slopes. Also, because south-facing slopes are more exposed to the evaporating influence of the sun, they are drier than north-facing slopes.

In eastern forests, in general, south-facing slopes have southern affinity species, such as oaks and hickories, while the north-facing slopes have northern affinity species, such as beech and sugar maple. Exceptions to this pattern can exist where a spring brings moisture to a dry slope or where a relatively flat hollow or cove collects moisture that has traveled down a steep slope.

In the Catoctin Mountains, large stands of conifers, especially eastern hemlocks, are found in ravines and along stream beds in the cool, moist soils—particularly on shady, north-facing slopes (Figure 59).

Figure 59. From Chimney Rock looking south in winter. Below, in moist areas, on the north slope of the Hunting Creek valley, hemlocks grow across a wide area.

Previous Human Activity and Fire

Events that remove or destroy the forest create a barren environment for succession to begin again. Initially, for several years following a disturbance, pioneer plants such as locust and pine are the ones that prosper. However, the decades needed to re-establish the climax forest can be lost in the destruction of clear-cutting or a fire. For example, the slope to the east of Park Central Road from the Visitor Center to the Thurmont Vista parking lot was burned about 1940; as a result, today the trees are smaller there than those of other areas. Fire can be beneficial, however, because it usually generates greater diversity in the forest.

Nearly all of the Catoctin forests have been cut one or more times. The continuous supply of wood needed for the iron furnaces was gathered by clear-cutting a section of the forest each year and returning to that section for another cutting every 25 to 35 years. Natural succession was altered because stumps were left. After being cut the American chestnuts and the oaks, which both have excellent stump-sprouting capability, were able to return and be the dominant species for their brief lifetimes. Evidence of stump-sprouting since the last cutting can still be seen in many areas of the Catoctins today (Figures 60 and 61).

Figure 60. This tree, next to the trail to Cat Rock (probably an old logging road) likely was cut for timber years ago. It has regenerated itself by double sprouting.

Invading Organisms

Alien organisms, plant or animal, and alien substances, usually human-introduced, can cause destruction or near-extinction of particular native species and alter the overall species composition of the forest.

Chestnut Blight

Probably the most dramatic example of forest disturbance by an alien organism is the chestnut blight. At the beginning of the twentieth century, the Catoctin and many other eastern forests consisted of about 50 percent American chestnut trees. This tall, fast-growing tree produced wood that was widely used for building, and it provided nuts that were eaten by wild animals and humans.

In 1906, a fungus that was probably introduced from eastern Asia infested chestnut trees in the New York City area. The fungus disease spread quickly, attacking the unresistant chestnuts. The disease reached the Catoctins in about 1912 and by the 1940s had killed most of the large chestnut trees. The oak-chestnut forest type became the oak-hickory forest as hickories moved in to replace the chestnuts.

Today chestnuts in the Catoctins exist only in the understory, as shoots from the blight-resistant roots (Figure 62). By the time they reach about 20 feet in height, the blight usually kills them. A few chestnuts may still be present in the Chestnut Picnic Area, where a restoration project of four years' length was abandoned in the early 1990s because many of the trees had succumbed to the blight (Figure 63).

Figure 61. This double-sprouter on Bobs Hill is also doing a major job of root wedging in the rock.

74

Figure 62. The small spikes or hooks along the edges are distinctive of the American chestnut leaf. Young chestnuts grow along the trail near Cat Rock.

Gypsy Moth

Today hickories, maples and especially oaks are threatened by the gypsy moth caterpillar. Brought to Massachusetts from Europe during the 19th century, the gypsy moth was observed in the Catoctins in the early 1980s. Research in the early 1990s indicated that the spread of the leaf-eating moths had been accelerated by human activities during the previous couple of decades to a rate almost ten times that of natural spread. The larvae disperse quickly by hitching rides on recreational vehicles, moving vans, transported plants and firewood.

Because the gypsy moth is a non-native species, it is not as yet held in check by natural predators or parasites. In addition, it is hardy and prolific: each tiny egg has a thick, protective shell, and the egg mass contains a large number of eggs. The caterpillars, which hatch from the eggs in late

75

April or early May, are ravenous consumers of the leaves of hardwoods, especially the oaks. The caterpillars feed for up to two months before maturing into moths, which do not feed on leaves. Trees that have been defoliated and killed are visible from some trails (Figures 64).

Figure 63. At the restoration area the chestnut in the center foreground, growing about as tall as most ever get—nearly thirty feet—is showing signs along its central trunk of being badly blighted. It will soon be dead.

Catoctin Mountain Park has been involved with the monitoring, trapping and suppression of the moth since 1982. Large areas have been sprayed with Bt, *Bacillus thuringiensis*, a natural bacteria that paralyzes the digestive system of the gypsy moth. In summer 1990 an aerial detection flight revealed no visible defoliation. When later egg mass surveys showed low levels, no spraying was done from 1991 through 1993. Continued close monitoring and spraying should control the infestation in the future.

Gypsy moth damage in Cunningham Falls State Park was more widespread than in Catoctin Mountain Park. The state park did conduct spraying in the early 1990s.

Figure 64. A chestnut oak defoliated by gypsy moth caterpillars, visible from the top of Bobs Hill.

Gypsy moth traps are visible from many trails in Catoctin Mountain Park. Visitors should not disturb these traps or handle any caterpillars found. Contact with the caterpillar, which can be identified by the double row of spots down its back, can cause a skin rash on some persons.

Dogwood Anthracnose

The harbinger of spring, the flowering dogwood (*Cornus florida*), is now seriously threatened throughout the northern and southern Appalachian regions by a fungus called anthracnose (Figure 65). This fungal disease was first reported in the parks in 1983. Initial symptoms include purple-

Figure 65. This dogwood along Route 77 has blossoms on its upper branches, but the lower limbs—just below the lowest wire—have died (spring 1994).

rimmed spots and large brown blotches on the leaves, twig die back, and lower branch die back. Eventually the tree dies. Infection increases in cool, wet springs or falls.

As of spring 1991 about 80 percent of the dogwoods in Catoctin Mountain Park had been killed, and by summer 1993 the percentage had risen to 95 to 98 percent. Research is presently being conducted in the park to develop a strain of dogwood that is resistant to the fungus.

Why Do Leaves Change Color and Fall?

During spring and summer, green chlorophyll in leaves manufactures sugars and starches for the tree through photosynthesis. In fall the rate of chlorophyll renewal declines and its green color begins to fade. Other pigments—present in the leaves throughout the growing season—begin to show their colors as the chlorophyll fades.

Orange comes from carotenoids, pigments that are also responsible for the color in carrots and pumpkins. Yellow comes from xanthophylls, pigments that are also responsible for the color in squash and lemons. Red comes from anthocyanin, a pigment that is manufactured after the chlorophyll disappears. The color intensity of anthocyanin depends on the amount of sugar produced in the leaves during the fall. Thus, leaves on the sunny side of a tree are usually brighter than those on the shady side.

With cool temperatures during fall, photosynthesis slows down, and the leaves become less efficient at producing food for the tree. At the base of the leaf stalk, a thin layer of cells—the abscission layer—begins to grow. The orange, yellow, or red pigments appear, but eventually the abscission layer cuts the leaf off from the tree. The many leaves that fall then decay and contribute minerals and nutrients into the soil.

Spring Wildflowers

The great diversity of flowering plants is a testament to one of the most important developments of evolution: sexual reproduction. By mixing characteristics from two different parents in successive generations, sexual reproduction yields a variety of traits in offspring populations. This variety helps to protect the species against extinction should environmental conditions change.

Genetic information is contained in pollen, and wildflower pollen is transported by insects. With a color, pattern or scent that attracts an insect, a flower is so designed that its pollen will rub off on the visitor, who is rewarded with nectar. When the insect visits the blossom of another plant, the pollen from the previous plant is deposited and pollination occurs.

During March, April and May, depending on the weather and elevation, the wildflowers bloom in profusion at certain locations in the parks. Most wildflowers need the rays of the sun to grow and bloom, so many of them complete their above-ground cycles before the emerging tree leaves cause the forest floor to be shaded.

Please DO NOT PICK WILDFLOWERS—doing so is against the law because it endangers their existence.

Wildflowering Locations

The parks have several easily accessible locations where visitors can enjoy a rich variety of flowers without walking too far. Several locations are accessible to persons with disabilities. Early to mid-April is a good time to start looking, and it is an intimate way to participate in the rebirth of spring. Purchase a wildflower book if you wish, or just go look.

• **Near the road bridge on the flat above Cunningham Falls, about ¾ mile inside the parks from the west entrance on Route 77.**

Park alongside Route 77 near the bridge over Hunting Creek, above and to the west of the falls, and explore the banks of the creek.

Skunk cabbage is the first plant to emerge—often during March—with the delicate spring beauty soon after. Here can also be found toothwart, rue anemone, wood anemone, yellow violet, dwarf ginseng, yellow adder's tongue, hepatica and more.

• **Trail to Cunningham Falls**

The trail from the parking area on Route 77 to the falls—accessible to those with disabilities—affords opportunity to see many of the species listed above, but the area is heavily trampled, and few plants grow well on hard-packed ground. Flowers grow around the bases of trees, in the underbrush and near stream banks. Most of these locations are visible from the trail.

• **Gravel parking lot across Park Central Road from Visitor Center**

This area is a good place for the novice flower-hunter to start because many species can be seen within a relatively small area. Follow the trail marked "Cunningham Falls" for a few hundred feet over the footbridge and to the base of the hillslope. Check the bases of the trees along the trail and walk carefully along the edges of the small stream that flows beneath the footbridge. Throughout this area are beautiful clusters of mixed species.

In addition, flowers can be seen growing in the flat woods just adjacent to the parking lot and up along the Blue Blazes Still Trail, although the diversity may not be as rich here.

• **Along Hunting Creek below Visitor Center**

The many roadside pull-offs and parking spaces provide access to good wildflowering locations near the banks and on the flood plain of Hunting Creek.

• **Brown's Farm Trail**

Beginning at the first parking lot at Owens Creek Picnic Area, this 0.4 mile loop trail is relatively flat. It passes through a moist area that is home to skunk cabbage, jack-in-the-pulpit, adder's tongue, spring beauties and many others.

• **Wildflower Walks**

During April and May, Catoctin Mountain Park sponsors wildflower walks on Saturdays and Sundays. Call the visitor center or check local newspapers for the times and dates.

By late May or early June the flowers' blossoms are gone, so do not delay in making your visit.

Picking the flowers is against the law and would rob others of pleasure, not to mention the damage it would do to the plant community. Photographing individual plants or blossoms usually requires a close-up lens, but good "group shots" can be taken by getting as close as your camera will allow. Be careful where you step so that you do not crush the delicate flowers.

A few of the many spring wildflowers are pictured below.

Figure 66. Relative of the rue anemone, the *wood anemone* has a whorl of three-stalked, deeply cut leaves. Because their slender stalks allow them to fritter in the breeze, anemones are also known as wind flowers.

Figure 67. A true member of the violet family, the *yellow violet* reveals on close inspection that its stalk is softly hairy.

81

Figure 68. The *great chickweed* has five petals that are deeply cut and give the first appearance of being ten. The leaves are oblong and opposite. Here the chickweed grows next to a *mayapple* "umbrella."

Figure 69. By mid-summer most of the forest floor is shaded by the tree leaves above, and the wildflowers' blossoms are gone. At this time *Ferns* cover most of the forest floor.

Wildlife and Animal Habitats

Wildlife Populations

The forests and streams of the two parks offer rich habitats for many animals and birds. Animals most likely to be observed by the park visitor are deer, squirrel, chipmunk, raccoon, skunk, opossum and fox.

Mammals

The *grey squirrel* resides in the oak-hickory forest, where it forages for food during early morning and late afternoon. It eats nuts, acorns, seeds, berries, tree buds, mushrooms and bark. Working through the leaves, the grey squirrel buries food at different locations in the ground by using its dexterous forepaws. The grey squirrel builds a leaf nest either in the hollow trunk of a tree or in the bough of a tree.

On higher slopes and ridges lives the *red squirrel*. It will inhabit areas with evergreens, where it may build an outside nest. The red squirrel will hoard its food and locate its stash in one place.

At night the seldom-seen *flying squirrel* glides from tree to tree on the wing-like folds of skin that are stretched taut from fore to hind legs. This animal is very adept at gliding but is not capable of true flight. It has large, sensitive eyes and makes a chirping sound. The scratching, scurrying sound of the squirrel's landing on a tree trunk can sometimes be heard.

A member of the squirrel family, the *chipmunk* may sound its warning cluck when an intruder nears and if threatened will disappear down the opening of its burrow in the ground. The chipmunk's diet is varied but includes mostly nuts, berries and seeds. Its call of "chock, chock, chock" can often be heard. Like other small mammals it has many predators and has thus developed quick, darting evasive movements.

The *raccoon* is usually nocturnal and eats just about anything—often the food that campers leave out or morsels found in garbage cans. Its dexterous paws enable it to acquire food from these containers, but the raccoon also rolls over stream rocks to look for crayfish or aquatic insects, or turns logs on land to look for salamanders. The raccoon lives in a cavity in the trunk of a tree, high up. Raccoons are particularly to be avoided in the wild because they are susceptible to rabies during the peak years of that disease and can quickly transmit it to humans through a bite.

The *skunk* defends itself with a pungent, malodorous spray, but it can be observed safely if approached quietly and not too closely. Its black-and-white striped coat is associated with the powerful odor by many potential predators. The skunk lives in an abandoned ground burrow, or perhaps a hollow log, and seeks food by rooting for insects or grubs. It is not quick or agile because it usually does not need to run.

Figure 70. When snow covers the ground and a partially frozen stream, animal tracks can be found.

The *opossum* is slow in movement and reaction, and it will "play possum," or pretend to be dead if threatened. It eats just about anything, including carrion and garbage, and lives in hollow trees or logs, many of which were previously inhabited by other animals. If surprised, it will often climb a tree, where it can be observed. The opossum, unfortunately, is often the victim of vehicle traffic.

At dusk the *bat* emerges from a hollow tree, cave or old building and flies about, consuming insects. The only mammal capable of true flight, the bat navigates by emitting its own kind of radar: high-pitched clicks that bounce off objects and return to the bat's ears for interpretation of locations. Many humans fear—perhaps because of Hollywood productions—that bats are "creepy" or will attack, but their sophisticated guidance system is used to avoid objects and to find insects for food. There is very little danger of a bat's colliding with a human.

At night the *mice* come out from their holes in logs, rocks and leaves to scour the forest floor for seeds, berries, grasses and insects. They forage at night to help avoid their many predators—including snakes, hawks and owls. Because many are taken, many young are reproduced to assure species survival.

Snakes

Several species of non-venomous snakes can be observed in the park, but two kinds of venomous snakes are occasionally seen: the *copperhead* and the *timber rattlesnake*. Some visitors may avoid the woods because of these two, but encounters are rare.

Copperheads and rattlers do not lie in wait beside the trail to lunge at the shins and ankles of unsuspecting hikers. Their habitat includes rocky slopes, loose rock walls, stream areas and abandoned buildings or wood-piles. For the hiker the best precautions are looking before walking and keeping hands away from cracks and crevasses in rocks.

The copperhead and the timber rattlesnake differ in appearance from other snakes in the area in that the poisonous snakes have thin necks and triangular heads. The copperhead is tan and thus well camouflaged on the forest floor. It may bite if stepped on, but it is primarily a night stalker and is seldom seen during daylight. The timber rattler is yellow through brown or gray or black, with irregular black bands and blotches that are chevron or diamond shaped. At tail's end is the rattler, which may sometimes—but not always—provide a warning to stay away with a kind of high frequency vibrato hissing sound. Rocky outcrops are a favorite habitat, and during spring and fall it is active during the day. The main food of these two snakes is rodents.

Deaths from timber rattler bites are very rare nationwide, and deaths from copperhead bites are almost unknown.

Three varieties of non-venomous snakes inhabit the parks: the *black rat snake* and the *ring-necked snake*. Near streams the *water snake* lives. As with venomous snakes, encounters are rare.

Birds

Many different bird species have been observed in the park. A check-list of 140 birds observed in Catoctin Mountain Park is available at the Visitor Center.

Commonly found birds include American woodcock, killdeer, broad-winged hawk, turkey vulture, wild turkey, morning dove, barred owl, eastern screech owl, great horned owl, downy woodpecker, pileated woodpecker, red-bellied woodpecker, northern flicker, American crow, blue jay, brown-headed cowbird, common grackle, northern oriole, wood thrush, veery, American robin, blue-gray gnatcatcher, gray catbird, northern mock-ingbird, red-eyed vireo, yellow-throated vireo, great crested flycatcher, eastern phoebe, eastern wood pewee, house wren, carolina chickadee, tufted titmouse, white-breasted nuthatch, black-and-white warbler, Kentucky warbler, yellow warbler, Louisiana waterthrush, American redstart, common yellowthroat, ovenbird, northern cardinal, American goldfinch, house finch, purple finch American tree sparrow, chipping sparrow, field sparrow, house sparrow, song sparrow, white-throated sparrow, dark-eyed junco, rufous-sided towhee, indigo bunting, scarlet tananger, European starling, ruby-throated hummingbird, chimney swift and belted kingfisher.

The destruction of the understory by the overly large deer herd has had a detrimental effect on many birds. For example, there have been fewer sightings of grouse, which rely on understory thickets for cover. In addition, populations of wild turkey are never very abundant because turkey are in direct competition with deer for food.

Surprisingly, during 1990, one adult bald eagle and one immature golden eagle were sighted migrating through the area.

Fish and Aquatic Life

Big Hunting Creek is stocked by the state with hatchery-reared rainbow trout and brook trout. Brown trout naturally reproduce in this stream. Big Hunting Creek is open year-round for fishing and is managed as a fly-fishing-only, catch-and-release, no-kill area.

Owens Creek is managed for native brook and for naturally producing brown trout. As of January 1, 1991, stocking of rainbow trout was stopped in Catoctin Park, and there are no longer any rainbows in the sections of Owens Creek that run through Catoctin Mountain Park. There is little fishing pressure on Owens Creek; there are no tackle restrictions but the limit is two per day.

A short section of Little Hunting Creek that lies within Cunningham Falls Park at the Manor Area is open to fishing.

Figure 71. Winter fishing—more aesthetic than productive.

Minnow species present in the streams include blacknose dace, longnose dace, rosyside dace, white sucker, mottled sculpin and fantail darter. Also present is the American eel.

In the protected crannies of the gravel bottoms of these fast streams are insect larvae, which are food for the fish. Aquatic life is rich here because the flowing water brings plenty of dissolved oxygen. Attached to the sides or bottoms of stones can be found mayfly nymph, hellgrammite, caddisfly larvae, stonefly nymph and water penny (aquatic beetle).

Trout feed on the larval, pupal and adult stages of mayflies, stoneflies, caddisflies and midges. They also feed on crayfish, dace and sculpin. However, from late spring through early fall, terrestrial insects that fall into the stream, such as beetles, flies, ants and grasshoppers, contribute more to trout diet than aquatic forms.

Fishing in the Parks

Big Hunting Creek Lake in Cunningham Falls State Park is stocked with rainbow trout and also has largemouth bass. Boats with electric motors up to one horsepower are permitted on the lake. A boat ramp is located off Catoctin Hollow Road on the southeast side of the lake, and no park entry fee is needed to use it.

Big Hunting Creek (also called Hunting Creek) is one of the best trout streams in Maryland. With natural brown trout and stocked brooks and rainbows, the stream is a special catch-and-return area. This area includes the tributaries of Big Hunting Creek within the two parks, and its special regulations are as follows:

1. All trout must be released to the water.
2. Fishing may be done only with artificial flies, including streamers, with single hooks.
3. Fishing must be done with conventional fly fishing tackle. Any method of angling by which the fly is cast directly from the reel is prohibited.
4. Possession of any bait or lures other than artificial flies is prohibited.
5. Open season: January 1 through December 31, inclusive.

Big Hunting Creek roughly parallels Route 77, which has numerous parking pull-offs for fishermen. A paved area just below the Visitor Center on Route 77 has room for over 15 vehicles. Near the Administrative Office, there are large parking areas on each side of the creek. Near the mouth of Bear Branch are a few wide pull-offs. Other smaller pull-offs are along Route 77.

Below the lake, down to Frank Bentz Pond at the eastern park boundaries, is probably the best section to fish. The stream is a series of pools and riffles—some natural and some the result of jack dams and deflector structures built to enhance trout habitat. It runs beneath a beautiful canopy of hardwoods and conifers, and because of its narrow width of 10 to 20 feet, only short casts are needed. Because the trout are shy, the pools should be approached carefully to prevent spooking the fish.

Owens Creek is accessible from Route 550 (the road from Thurmont to Sabillisville) and from Foxville-Deerfield Road in the western section of Catoctin Mountain Park. It is managed for native brook and brown trout, and is no longer stocked inside Catoctin Park with rainbows. The limit is two fish per day, with any type of bait and tackle allowed. It's good to check regulations because Owens Creek closes periodically, and the opening day varies yearly.

In addition, Little Hunting Creek is a stocked, put-and-take trout stream, and a section of it is accessible from the lower picnic area of the Cunningham Falls Park Manor Area.

These creeks have good aquatic insect populations. For fly-fishing, the following hatch information may be helpful.

1. Little Black Stonefly—very good hatch but small flies (sizes 18 to 22) should be used. Late February to late March.
2. Blue Quill—sizes 16 to 18. Mid- to late March.
3. Larger Stonefly, Hendrickson, Quill Gordon—April 15–May 15.
4. March Brown—early May to mid-May.
5. Light Cahill—mid-May to early June.
6. Caddis—very small flies; most are dark. April and May.
7. Terrestrials—late May through summer. Ants, beetles and a small, bright green inchworm are good.

A Maryland fishing license is required, and state regulations apply for all of these areas. A Maryland trout stamp is required to fish in the catch-and-release, no-kill area and to possess trout in the put-and-take areas.

Deer and the Forest

Since the early 1990s one of the big problems for Catoctin Mountain Park has been overpopulation by whitetail deer. The 1992 estimated herd size of about 550 was far too large for an area that can reasonably support about 150 to 190. The harsh winter of 1993 reduced that estimate to about 260. Overpopulation results in problems both for the deer and for the vegetation on which they feed.

During winter, the large herd consumes most of the readily available food. When the food runs low, the starved and skinny deer become too weak to run and have difficulty moving through the snow to the food that

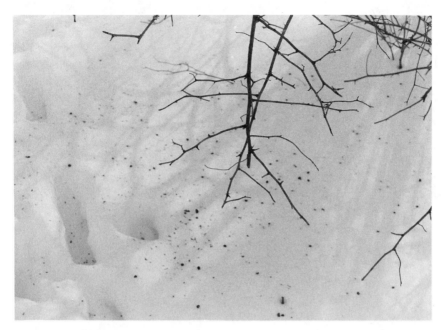

Figure 72. During hard winters, deer are forced to eat any available small branches.

remains (Figure 72). Many deer starve or freeze to death. Numerous deer necropsies have revealed little or no fat tissue on internal organs and in bone marrow. Particularly vulnerable to starvation are the younger and the older deer. Surviving does give birth to single fawns instead of twins, and most bucks have small racks—both indicators of malnutrition and hunger.

The forest suffers in many ways from deer overpopulation. An obvious indicator of the presence of too many deer is the browse line, a plane through the forest, about 5 to 6 feet high, under which most of the vegetation has been eaten. This line is as high as deer can reach with their mouths. In some places the forest floor is vacant of understory—the shrubs, ferns, young trees and tall herbs normally found in the shade beneath the taller, mature trees. In many areas of the park, either the browse line or the depletion of the understory can be seen from the road (Figure 73).

Many beautiful mountain laurel and rhododendron in Catoctin Park have been chewed off up to the browse line or, in some places, almost completely eaten by the deer. Damage to these plants indicates severe conditions because they represent starvation food—food of very little nutrition that is eaten when the deer may be too weak to move very far in search of better food.

Another kind of damage occurs when deer strip bark from elm trees during winter. Near Owens Creek Campground is the heaviest concentration of this tree damage. Parkwide, over 200 elms have been stripped during the last decade. Unprotected, the trees are invaded by a fungus that quickly kills them.

Figure 73. From Park Central Road, the browse line is evident in the lack of understory and of lower tree limbs.

Yet another loss is that of rare plants and wildflowers. Of eleven rare plant species identified in a 1985 study, all but two have disappeared. The two that remain—purple fringed orchids and leatherwood shrub—have been considered since the early 1990s as "highly rare," a category close to "endangered." Found along Owens Creek near the campground, these two species are now being protected from browsing by small wire cages that are placed around individual plants. Other species that have diminished or disappeared are columbine, cardinal flower and pink and yellow lady slipper.

Thus, the deer are changing many plant populations in the park. Studies with ten-meter-square exclosures—structures that fence deer out—have dramatically illustrated that if an area is fenced during the growing season and thus left unbrowsed, the abundance and diversity of species increases markedly within the exclosures.

In adjacent Cunningham Falls State Park, where hunting is permitted in some areas, the understory is in generally better condition than in overbrowsed Catoctin Park. (See Trail Guide for the Dam-to-Cat Rock hike). Mountain laurel, sprouting American chestnut and ferns abound in some sections (Figure 74).

The deer often take refuge in Catoctin Park soon after the hunting starts in the state park; thus, the Catoctin Park population increases dramatically during the first few days of hunting season. Such movement may be one factor contributing to the overbrowsing in Catoctin Park, even though some deer may return to the state park after the season.

In addition to the problems within Catoctin Park, deer move out of the park at night to feed in nearby orchards and farm fields—as is evidenced by increased complaints from land owners. The deer return to the sanctuary of the park before sun-up, the time when it becomes legal for farmers and orchardists to shoot deer to protect their crops.

Park rangers have been faced with the fact that the herd must be reduced in order to save the forest floor and to prevent cruel deaths by starvation. The most obvious and most often suggested solution—to open the area to hunting—is not feasible: an act of Congress would be required to reverse the original no-hunting restriction established for the Catoctin Demonstration Area.

Many other solutions have been discussed: trapping and relocating, sterilizing of does, increasing the deer harvest outside of the park, re-introducing predators, enclosing the deer with fences, and direct reduction by park personnel. Another option—the one presently being followed—is to take no action, and let the herd control its own numbers. The hard winter of 1993 reduced the herd by about one-half.

Catoctin Park is not the only area where deer overpopulation is a problem, and many reasons have been advanced for the widespread population increases. Deer prefer a forest-edge habitat; increased commercial and residential development over the past few decades has broken up and divided the forest, thereby creating more edge habitat. Also, the mildness

Figure 74. Rich understory can be found along many trails in Cunningham Falls State Park, where hunting of deer is permitted in some areas.

of the winters of the 1980s and early 1990s may have allowed more and more deer to survive. Finally, land around Catoctin Park is less hunted and more heavily posted than in previous decades; thus, the hunting pressure has been reduced.

Even if the herd size is reduced, re-establishment of the understory would be a difficult task. Experimental plots indicate that in some parts there is very little regeneration. The forest may not have the diversity it had 20 years ago—wildflowers, rhododendron, azalea and mountain laurel. However, the forest has often regenerated itself from other forces of change, such as fire, logging and farming; it is reasonable to assume that, in the long term, it can recover from the damage by deer as well.

Figure 75. A deer crosses Park Central Road in Catoctin Mountain Park near Camp Greentop and Chestnut Picnic Area.

Human History

Indians

The ancestors of American Indians crossed the land bridge that is today the Bering Strait from Asia about 14,000 years ago during the Ice Age. In the Middle Atlantic region, Indian habitation and culture is usually divided into three periods: Paleo-Indian (11,000–8,000 BC); Archaic (8,000–1,000 BC); and Woodland (1,000 BC–AD 1600). Evidence indicates that Indians were present during each of these periods in the Catoctins or the Frederick Valley.

As the Ice Age glaciers retreated, the Paleo-Indians reached the middle Atlantic area about 11,000 BC. They were hunters and gatherers who followed herds of now-extinct prehistoric animals. The presence of these skilled hunters is indicated by finds in Frederick County that include hunting instruments and a mastodon tooth.

During the Archaic period, temperatures gradually increased and vegetation grew more abundantly. Human population gradually increased, and more seasonal and semi-permanent settlement developed. Seasonal movement and the development of trade gave rise to Indian paths that criss-crossed the region. Just north of the Catoctins, in Pennsylvania, quar-

Figure 76. Arrowheads found in the Hagerstown Valley probably came from the metarhyolite of south-central Pennsylvania or the Catoctins. These arrowheads are from the collection of Mike Wilson, Hagerstown, Maryland.

ries of Archaic age have been found in the metarhyolite rock near Jacks Mountain and near Caledonia State Park. Stone tools and projectile points were fashioned from this metavolcanic rock, the same formation which runs through the western part of Catoctin Mountain Park (Figure 76). Tools made of metarhyolite points have been found as far away as the eastern shore of Chesapeake Bay.

When white men arrived on the continent in the early 1600s, the Indians had been in the area that is now Maryland for over 12,000 years. During the early 1600s the area that is now between Washington DC, Baltimore, South Mountain and the Susquehanna River was controlled by the powerful Susquehannoughs, although evidence that any band of Indians ever had a permanent home in the Catoctins has not been found. During this time, the Patuxent and the Piscataway, tribes living downstream on the Potomac River near Chesapeake Bay, probably traveled up the river to the Catoctins for winter hunting. Early settlers in this area claimed that an Indian hunting camp was located a short distance northwest of Frederick.

By 1700 the area that is now Frederick County had become an unsettled middle ground due to Indian wars and to resettlement caused by the white man's influence. In fact, in 1652 the Susquehannoughs ceded their land west of the Chesapeake to Lord Baltimore, who claimed land as far west as the Allegheny Mountains for Maryland.

Early Settlers

The first settlers in the Frederick County area came not from the east but from the north, through Pennsylvania, and they followed Indian paths. In the early 1700s Germans migrated westward from Philadelphia along the Great Minqua Path, which roughly paralleled present-day US Route 30. After crossing the Susquehanna River, they followed the Monocacy Path near the present-day sites of York, Hanover and Taneytown and into the valley of the Monocacy River east of the Catoctins.

By the 1730s, when white settlers began arriving in what is now Frederick County, the Indians had already left the area. In March 1732, Lord Baltimore proclaimed that for the next three years settlers in this area could receive 200 acres of their own choosing, free for three years and with minimal rent thereafter. Thus, the land here was uncontested and essentially free.

Two of the earliest families to settle in the Catoctin Mountains were second-generation German-American: Fox and Bussard. The present community of Foxville, near the intersection of Stottlemeyer Road and Route 77, is the namesake of George P. Fox, Sr., who acquired much land in the area of Round Meadow and the northwestern section of Catoctin Mountain Park.

"Cunningham Falls" and 350 acres surrounding it were purchased on September 16, 1807, by Archibald McAfee, Sr. The McAfee family lived

Figure 77. Reuben McAfee, grandson of Archibald McAfee, at the top of the falls with the McAfee family (from Wireman, 1969).

near the top of the falls, and the original foundation of the homestead still stands (Figure 77). The family owned the land until it was acquired by the Federal government in 1935. The falls were never owned by anyone named Cunningham and were known as McAfee Falls until the 1940s or the early 1950s.

Early Trades, Industries and Travel

Sawmills

Lumbering and sawmills were lucrative businesses in the mountains in the 19th century. As many as ten up-and-down sawmills operated in the Catoctins before the Civil War.

The reconstructed sawmill near Owens Creek Campground (see Trail Guide, Sawmill Trail, and Figure 78) is a typical example of a mill where the long cutting blades moved up and down. Running water from a stream was channeled into a trough, or raceway, to turn a water wheel. The wheel powered the sash, a wooden frame that held several large saw blades arranged in parallel fashion for the cutting of planks.

A deep trench, or saw pit, provided room for the vertical movement of the sash. The timber, anchored at ground level, was slowly advanced into the up-and-down cutting blades by mechanical devices. Operated by the

Figure 78. A reconstructed, 19th century up-and-down sawmill is located near Owens Creek Campground.

sawyer and the pitman, a sawmill produced only about 48 planks during a twelve-hour work day.

Tanneries

In 1810 Frederick County had almost 50 tanneries, most of them farm-sized operations. Tanners changed hides into leather by soaking them in pits of tanning liquor made from the tannic acid that was abundantly available in the bark of chestnut, chestnut oak and hemlock.

Stripping bark from trees in the mountains was yet another huge demand made on the forest. In fact, by the 1850s one tanner, Daniel Rouzer, had to get his bark from nearby Pennsylvania mountains because the Catoctins had been nearly depleted by the tanning, lumbering and iron/charcoal operations.

Roads

Authorized in 1810 by the state legislature, privately financed builders constructed a road that followed an old Indian path through Harmon's Gap—present-day Hunting Creek valley. Completed in 1816, the road connected Hagerstown and Westminster. It was known as the Westminster-Hagerstown Pike and today is Maryland State Route 77. The original mountain dirt road was once one of America's main routes toward the west because it joined the National Road (Route 40) at Hagerstown. It was not paved until 1947.

Whiskey

Distillation of rye and corn solutions into liquor probably took place on most Frederick County farms during the 1700s; however, the 1791 excise tax took the profit out of making whiskey for even personal consumption. Because mere ownership of a still was taxable, whiskey makers worked in secret or by the light of the moon, making "moonshine." The reconstructed distillery near the creek up the hollow from the Visitor Center is typical of the early still (see Trail Guide, Blue Blazes Whiskey Still Trail and Figure 79).

During Prohibition years, however, large quantities of booze were distilled on this site by a larger, more elaborate operation. Operation ceased on the last day of July 1929, when a raid closed down the distillery. Found by the deputies that day were 13 vats holding more than 25,000 gallons of mash.

Figure 79. The reconstructed whiskey still.

History of Catoctin Furnace

The industry that affected the Catoctin Mountains the most significantly and for the longest time was ironmaking. With the furnaces in operation at the base of the mountains from 1776 to 1903, the forests were heavily logged for charcoal to fire the furnaces, and pits were dug at the base of the mountains for iron ore. Today a restored furnace stands just off Route 15 south of the Manor Area of Cunningham Falls State Park.

Ironmaking in Colonial America

The first two furnaces at Catoctin were probably typical of those found in eleven of the thirteen colonies. The blast furnace, or stack, common in the colonies in the middle of the 1700s was 25 to 35 feet high and about 25 feet square at the base, tapering to a slightly smaller square at the top. The exterior was of stone or brick; the interior chamber was of fire brick, with a soil-rock rubble chamber in between. The inner chamber, shaped somewhat like an inverted soda bottle, was open at the top, or throat, for the loading of the charge of charcoal, ore, and limestone. A few feet from the bottom was an air blast nozzle, through which air was blown into the furnace by a bellows worked by a water wheel. At the bottom was a channel through which the molten iron flowed out of the furnace into a series of parallel trenches for pig iron—so called because they resembled a sow nursing baby pigs—or into casting molds for pots, pans, kettles, stoves, tools, farm implements, shot or shells. The pig iron bars, measuring 5 to 6 feet by 6 inches, were further forged and refined, either on-site or elsewhere.

Putting "the stack into blast" was complicated, first requiring two fillings and burnings of charcoal without air blast. Then, with the cold air blast flowing to raise combustion temperatures, the fillers charged the furnace chamber with alternating layers of iron ore, limestone from local quarries, and charcoal.

In the different temperature zones of the furnace, these raw materials then underwent a number of chemical reactions:

1) Charcoal, composed of nearly pure carbon, was heated white-hot until it was oxidized by oxygen in the air to form carbon dioxide.

2) This carbon dioxide gas then combined with more carbon to form carbon monoxide gas.

3) The iron ore, an iron oxide, then reacted with the carbon monoxide to yield more carbon dioxide and molten, nearly pure iron, which was drawn from the furnace bottom.

4) The limestone—calcium carbonate—decomposed into calcium oxide, which then combined with the sand in the iron ore to form a glassy slag that was drawn from the bottom after the iron. In this way the silicon impurities in the ore were removed.

Development of the Catoctin Furnace

Since the 1600s, Great Britain had been the world's leading iron producer, but by 1775 about a seventh of the world's iron was produced by ironworks in the American colonies. When iron ore was discovered at the base of the Catoctin Mountains, all of the requirements for an iron furnace were met. The area already had vast woods for charcoal making, limestone rock for calcium carbonate, and fast-flowing streams for washing the ore and for providing mechanical power.

Catoctin Furnace became a major contributor to the prosperity of the iron industry in colonial days. From 1776 to 1903 the furnaces located here produced not only 80 to 100 pound bars of pig iron but also many specially cast items: cannon balls and cannon for Washington's Continental Army, machine parts for James Rumsey's steamboat—considered by many to be the first steamboat—and, it is believed by some, plates for the ironclad ship *Monitor*. Ore for the furnaces, in the form of limonite, an iron oxide, was dug from nearby pits at the base of Catoctin Mountain.

Early development of the industry was by the Johnson brothers, one of whom, Thomas, was the first governor of Maryland and a close friend of George Washington. The original patent for 7,000 acres—which included heavily wooded land where iron ore had been discovered—was obtained by Leonard Calvert and Thomas Johnson, but in 1774 Calvert transferred his interest to the other Johnson brothers: James, Roger and Baker. The

Figure 80. The ruins of Isabella, built in the late 1850s, as it appeared around 1895. The trapezoidal structure with the semi-circular opening at bottom is the actual stack or furnace. This furnace has been restored and can be visited (from Besley, 1922).

99

original furnace was built by James Johnson, an experienced ironmaster, and was located ¾-mile down Little Hunting Creek from the present site. It operated until 1787. Then the original Catoctin Furnace was built at the present site, which was closer to the ore banks. Each week the 32-foot high furnace produced 12 to 18 tons of pig iron, which was floated down the Monocacy River by Negro slaves (Figure 80).

By 1830, census tables showed an African-American slave population of 36 at Catoctin Furnace. Slaves were used throughout the western Maryland iron-making industry, and some of the furnace and charcoal technology may have been transferred here from African ironmaking.

The Johnsons operated or rented the industry until Baker's death in 1811. Two of the Johnson mansions—Springfield, built by James, and Auburn, by Baker—were located near present Route 15 not far from the furnace.

For the next century, the furnace had a series of owners. Some prospered more than others, but the furnace was in operation for most of those years. John Brien, owner from 1820 to 1834, made many improvements to the furnace property; after his wife Harriet's death in 1827, he built Harriet Chapel as a memorial to her. It still stands today, directly across from the furnace area. During this period the output of the furnace was still 12 to 18 tons per week.

Peregrine Fitzhugh, who operated the furnace from 1843 to 1858, built a new steam-powered hot-blast charcoal furnace, called Isabella (Figure 81), but the expense of it was too great and he sold out to John Kunkel.

Figure 81. The reconstructed Isabella is open to visitors during daylight hours. There is no admission.

Figure 82. Part of Catoctin Village, about 1900. At left is Catoctin House, the ironmaster's residence. Ruins of it still stand today (from Wireman, 1969).

Kunkel's two sons John and Jacob operated the furnace from 1859 to 1885. In 1873, a 50-foot high anthracite coal and coke furnace, Deborah, was erected, probably on the site of the original furnace, and the annual output was boosted to 1,200 tons of pig iron, nearly double that of earlier years. Also during Kunkel's ownership, Catoctin Furnace became a community, with saw and grist mills, 80 houses for workers and a company store (Figure 82). One hundred miners were on the Kunkel payroll, and in the mountain land, which had been expanded to 11,000 acres through Kunkel's purchase, about 300 woodchoppers and colliers worked.

For the remaining years, until 1903, the furnace was subject to falling iron prices and discontinuous operation. At one point a paint mill produced blue, red and yellow ochre from the clay found in the iron ore banks. Ore was hauled to Pennsylvania until 1912, nine years after the closing of the furnace.

Mining

Iron ore for the furnaces was obtained from three nearby sites, all located on the Catoctin property of over 10,000 acres. Behind the furnace were two ore banks, one 300' x 125' and another 500' x 100–150' (Figures 83 and 84). One-half mile south, behind Auburn, was a pit 500' x 200'. It was the very first to be opened, in 1774. A mile north of the furnace was the largest opening: 800' x 2,000'. The ore from this last pit was a good grade of limonite that occurred in lumps intermingled with a blue and yellow clay.

101

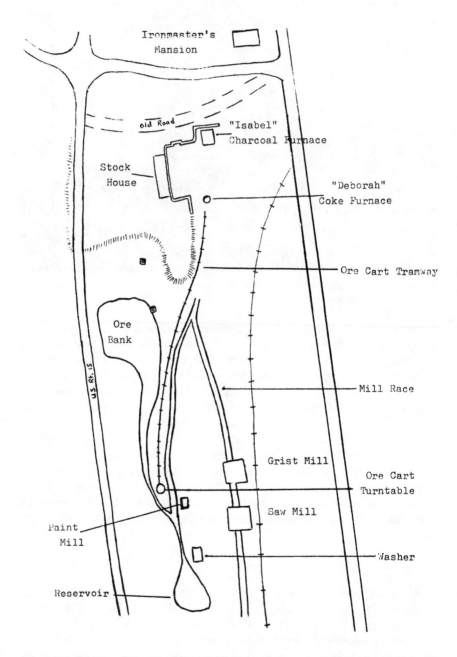

Figure 83. The overall layout of Catoctin Furnace shows one of the ore banks (from Thompson, 1976).

102

Figure 84. Catoctin Furnace in the late 1800s. Ore was hauled by rail from nearby ore pits to the furnace (from Wireman, 1969).

Washing was required to remove the ore, with seven tons of clay required to produce one ton of ore.

The ore was located along the Triassic Border Fault between the Harpers shale and the Frederick limestone. Possibly the shales produced iron-bearing solutions that washed down to the limestone and precipitated out of solution along the fault. In many places there was an overburden of more than ten feet of soil that had to be removed first.

The ore itself was considered a good chemical grade when it was mined, with analysis showing about a 40 percent content of the hydrous ferric oxide, limonite. The intense heat of the furnace was required to remove the oxygen and to make the iron melt and flow out in a relatively pure form.

The adjacent mountains were important also because they provided timber for charcoal and basins for stream systems. Charcoal provided heat for the process, while stream water was used for washing the ore and for driving the water wheel, which, in turn, operated the furnace bellows. As described above, limestone from nearby quarries was added to the ore in the furnace to serve as a flux to remove impurities. Air was then blasted into the furnace to cause the charcoal to reach higher temperatures.

Coaling

For almost its first 100 years of operation, the Catoctin Furnace used only charcoal for fuel—charcoal in prodigious amounts. Various estimates for the 18th century blast furnace are 800 bushels of charcoal per day, equivalent to 5,000–6,000 cords of wood per year or to an acre of 20- to 25-year-old hardwood timber per day. Thus, the furnace operation required large tracts of woodlands, as well as a large labor force of woodchoppers and charcoal burners (colliers) who lived and worked in the woods. The Kunkels, for instance, at one time employed about 300 choppers and colliers.

Woodland strips of hickory, oak, ash, chestnut and pine were felled systematically. Cut into 4-foot lengths and sorted by diameter, the wood was arranged into cords for purposes of payment. It was hauled on horse or mule-drawn half-cord sleds, always downhill, to the collier's hearth.

The hearth was a smooth, hard, flat space 30 to 40 feet in diameter and free of brush, roots and stones. Old hearths were periodically re-prepared and re-used as the 20 to 25 year cutting and regrowing cycle moved through the woods. Onto the hearth the woodhauler stacked the wood in a circle.

Figure 85. A stack of cut wood before being covered with leaves and dirt and fired by the collier to produce charcoal (National Park Service, Hopewell Furnace, Pennsylvania photo).

The collier then drove an 18-foot green pole into the center point and, working outward, carefully placed the four-foot logs end-on-end around the center pole into a cone-shaped stack about 25 feet in diameter and 4 to 6 feet high (Figure 85). A layer of leaves and dirt or charcoal dust was then plastered over the surface, but a small chimney was left at top center.

Firing the pit was done by placing a shovelful of hot coals onto kindling that had been arranged at the top of the chimney. The chimney was then carefully closed with leaves and dust, or with turf. The fire charred downward, and any sign of flame was quickly smothered because the intent was not to burn the wood but to smolder it and drive off its volatile compounds to leave charcoal of nearly pure carbon.

The pile or "pit" was constantly tended day and night by the collier and his helpers, who lived in wood huts erected nearby. Every three hours, the collier "jumped the stack"—he climbed onto the pile to settle charred wood and keep the pile tightly packed. Sometimes small holes were made to introduce air to certain parts, but great care was taken to prevent burning through, which could destroy the entire pile.

When the pile had completely charred down, the collier and his helpers carefully raked the still-hot charcoal into piles to cool. It was soon shoveled onto metal-lined charcoal wagons that were pulled by teams of horses to the charcoal house, a stone building located near the furnace.

An average hearth held 30 cords of wood and would produce almost 500 bushels of charcoal. Since nearly twice this amount was required by most blast furnaces for each day's operation, several piles had to be in process at one time.

Although the trees have been allowed to grow back for over 50 years, the marks of the charcoal production remain, both in the dirt roads that crisscross the mountains and in the still-visible hearths. The Charcoal Trail, which departs from the Thurmont Vista parking lot, has trail-side interpretive information about the charcoaling process and particular sites.

Catoctin Furnace—The Village

The village and buildings surrounding the furnace were an almost self-sufficient community. In 1820, there were 22 houses for workmen, but 40 years later during the Kunkel ownership there were 80, and other structures included a company store, a saw mill, a grist mill, and the ironmaster's house, the ruins of which are located just north of the furnace. An ore railroad supplied the three furnaces, and there were farms associated with the community. The Kunkels employed about 500 workers: 300 woodchoppers and colliers, 100 ore bank workers and 100 furnace workers. Above the village, 10,000 acres of mountain woodlands supplied the furnaces with fuel.

Catoctin Furnace and The Industrial Revolution

When the Johnsons first ventured their investment, America was mostly a rural, agrarian society. The large capital investment, the technological physical plant and the highly specialized work force were new, relatively revolutionary concepts in the colonies. The early furnaces were, then, forerunners of the industrial development that was to come to America later.

Ironically, the charcoal-fired iron industry was a rural rather than an urban enterprise. Because of limited transportation facilities, the furnace had to be located near the needed natural resources. However, the high cost of maintaining huge tracts of woodlands and a large labor force for the production of charcoal was the main reason for the installation of the coke furnace Deborah.

By the time it shut down in 1903, the furnace was outmoded and obsolete. It had been out-competed by corporation-owned industry that utilized improved iron-making technology, expanding transportation networks and large pools of urban workers.

The passing of Catoctin Furnace as a local industry was perhaps a harbinger of similar economic events of the mid-20th century: the passing of the neighborhood grocery, the local bakery, the local brewery. But also gone is the relatively isolated, unregulated industry whose owners and workers probably had little concern about environmental damage. An artist in a hot-air balloon could perhaps have painted an aerial picture of the 19th century furnace in full operation: continuous clouds of smoke rolling from the furnace stack, smoke rolling up from the colliers' stacks in the woods, bare mountain slopes denuded of trees, huge open pits of clay where ore was mined, and streams running muddy brown all the time with runoff from the bare mountain slopes, the open pits and the constant ore washing operations.

Figure 86. Catoctin Furnace in operation during late 19th century (Anderson, n.d.).

Park History and the Civilian Conservation Corps

Without President Franklin Roosevelt's New Deal program during the Depression, the Catoctin Mountains might still be an unprotected and abused forest area. In 1935 more than 10,000 acres were acquired by the Federal government, at $15 per acre, as an area in which to demonstrate the development of land unsuited for agricultural or commercial use into land conserved for recreation.

Catoctin was one of thirty-five areas in the Recreational Demonstration Area (RDA) Program. Nationally the goals of the RDA program were to:

1) acquire submarginal farm land or otherwise non-productive abused land;

2) resettle the inhabitants of the property;

3) put men to work by developing the "retired" land into recreation areas;

4) focus development on special use of the area by underprivileged children and families in nearby urban areas; and

5) overall, demonstrate uses of land for the greatest benefit to everybody.

The work was administered by the National Park Service, and the Catoctin project manager was G. B. "Mike" Williams. In April of 1935, the land acquisition began, with residents being relocated by agents of the Resettlement Administration.

Construction of Catoctin camp facilities began during the winter of 1936 and was done by WPA, the Works Progress Administration, a Roosevelt program that provided work for needy persons on public works projects of long-range value (Figure 87). The WPA concluded their work in 1941 with the Blue Blazes Contact Station, now known as the Visitor Center.

Figure 87. WPA built this blacksmith shop at Round Meadow in 1936. After the Recreational Demonstration Area was completed, it was used for occasional repair work. In the 1970s, Catoctin Park hosted a Folk Craft Center, and the blacksmith shop was one of the living history demonstrations.

Beginning in April 1939, work on roads, trails, stream improvements, reforestation and water systems was done by the Civilian Conservation Corps. This national agency was originally created in 1933 to provide work and training on conservation projects for unemployed, needy men between the ages of 18 and 25. While the CCC employed over two million nationwide, the Catoctin group comprised 300 workers.

Work in the mountains included improvement of six miles of existing country road, construction of three and a half miles of new road (the present Park Central Road) and fifty miles of foot and fire trails, and construction of three cabin-type group camps. Nearly all materials came from the mountains: 2,500,000 feet of blighted chestnut, other timber from areas cleared for roadways, and sand and rock from the stony slopes. Many materials were salvaged from farm buildings left in the area, and hinges and ironware were forged from scrap found in heaps.

Figure 88. A typical Misty Mount cabin.

As with many other CCC projects, the Catoctin work was designed to alleviate several problems or needs at once. It conserved the land; it trained and employed needy young men; it utilized existing materials; and it created outdoor recreation space for persons living in nearby crowded, urban areas. Specifically, the camps were for groups with educational programs that included camping and hiking.

Group Camp 1, Misty Mount, with 34 structures and a swimming pool, was opened in the late 1930s. The first group to be certified and to use the camp was the Baltimore League for Crippled Children and Adults. Over the years Misty Mount has been used by the Salvation Army, by the Girl

Scouts and by church and school groups; for example, during the 1960s and 1970s Washington County, Maryland, schools used the camp as its outdoor school for elementary school children. Today the cabins are open to the public if reserved in advance (Figure 88).

During the summer of 1937 Camp 2, Greentop, was opened. It was similar in design to Misty Mount, but the ground was flatter, being on the mountain top rather than on the slope. The Baltimore League moved to Greentop in 1937 and, except for the war years, has used it during the summers continuously ever since. Beginning in 1958, the Frederick County Outdoor Education School began holding its sessions during the school year at Greentop, thus providing the model for Washington County, which took up the idea beginning in 1960 at Misty Mount.

Camp 3, originally known as Hi-Catoctin (now under heavy security and closed to the public), was completed under a similar design during this period and was initially leased by a group of Washington government employees.

Round Meadow, in the western part of the park, served as the base camp for the WPA and CCC workers. Decades later, in the late 1960s, it served in a similar capacity for a descendant of CCC, President Johnson's Job Corps. This group constructed picnic areas, nature trails, a campground and a visitor center. Since the Job Corps left, Round Meadow has been used by DC schools as an outdoor camp. It is also the location of Catoctin Mountain Park's Resource Management Office.

During World War II, the three camps were used by the War Department for training purposes and for rest and recuperation. In the summer of 1942, however, President Roosevelt sought a secure rural retreat close to Washington for high-level conferences, for relaxation and for escape from the White House air conditioning, which he disliked.

When shown Hi-Catoctin, at an elevation of over 1800' and 10 to 15 degrees cooler than DC, he immediately liked it. The existing cabins were improved with conveniences, and a lodge was built for the President. Roosevelt named the camp "Shangri-La"; its existence was top-secret, except among suspicious residents of Thurmont, who told stories of automobile entourages speeding through town at 1 A.M. and of military guards standing beneath bridges. In 1945 it was revealed that Roosevelt and Churchill had met there several times to discuss strategy.

President Truman used the camp very little, but Eisenhower had improvements made and renamed it Camp David, after both his grandson and his father. President Eisenhower enjoyed outdoor grilling, fishing, hiking and golf at the camp, but he also held a cabinet meeting there, as well as a meeting with Soviet Premier Khrushchev.

The next President to have a strong attachment to Camp David was Eisenhower's running mate, Richard Nixon. President Nixon, according to one of his aides, would have moved in permanently had it been possible, and he often brought his staff there for intense discussions.

Camp David became internationally known in 1978 when talks there between President Carter, Egypt's President Anwar Sadat, and Israel's Prime Minister Menachem Begin produced the Camp David peace agreement.

The original intention of the Catoctin project in the 1930s was for the land to be transferred to the state of Maryland, but this was not accomplished until the mid-1950s, when about half of the total acreage, 4446 acres lying south of Route 77, were transferred to the state and became Cunningham Falls State Park. The remaining 5,770 acres lying north of Route 77 are Catoctin Mountain National Park.

In the late 1960s Big Hunting Creek Dam was built in the state park, the principal argument for its construction being that no good swimming location existed in Maryland between New Germany Park in Garrett County and Sandy Point on Chesapeake Bay. Today the area around the lake is known as the William Houck Area. Near the swimming beaches are campsites, boat rental, picnic tables, hiking trails and a snack bar. Today the lake is stocked and provides stillwater fishing, with electric motors of up to one horsepower permitted. Under an agreement reached in the 1960s, the dam provides a minimum base flow of 1.5 cfs for Hunting Creek, as well as a minimum of 5 ppm dissolved oxygen and a maximum temperature of 72°F.

Thanks to the government programs of the 1930s, the parks were allowed to become climax forests, in a preserve that is today nearly surrounded by the sprawling suburban development of the east.

Weather and Climate

Climate

"Climate" is a general description of prevailing weather conditions in a particular location, based on weather data collected over a long period of time. World climates are divided into about fifteen different types. The Catoctins are in the moist continental climate type—humid subtype—although they exhibit some characteristics of a highland climate.

The moist continental climate occurs over a large portion of midwestern, eastern and northeastern North America. This climate type lies in the latitudes where polar and tropical air masses meet and interact.

Precipitation

Precipitation in the Catoctins is distributed fairly evenly throughout the year. Annual precipitation is about 40 inches. Usually, slightly more precipitation occurs during summer than during winter. Summer rainfall is usually in the form of thunderstorms—moisture that is usually more variable in frequency and amount than that of winter storms. As a result, during summer streams can experience the sharpest rises and the lowest flows. For example, the summers of the late 1980s and early 1990s were very dry. Winter precipitation is often in the form of snow in the mountains, but during the late 1980s and early 1990s, snowfall was relatively light.

Effects of Changes in Elevation

For every 1,000-foot increase in elevation or altitude, the temperature decreases about 3.5°F—all other factors being equal. For example, if the temperature in Thurmont, at elevation 500 feet, is 80°F, Thurmont Vista, at 1,500 feet, would be about 76.5°F. Thus, the Catoctins, like other mountains, are cooler than nearby locations at lower elevations.

As a result, precipitation in the Catoctins is slightly higher—by a few inches per year—than it is in the Frederick Valley to the east. Most air masses approach on the prevailing north-westerly winds. When moist air ascends the western slopes, it can be cooled to the dew point—the temperature at which moisture condenses out of the air onto tiny particles in the air. This condensation can produce clouds, rain or snow—depending on temperature and humidity.

While this orographic cooling is not as marked in the Catoctins as it is in higher mountains, such as the Rockies, it does generate some local effects. Often the mountains are "in the clouds" (fog) when the valley is clear. (Clouds and fog both comprise water droplets suspended in air: clouds off the ground; fog near or in contact with the ground.) If the sun's rays warm the moisture in the air above the dew point, the water droplets

111

are vaporized back into the air—water vapor, itself, is invisible. The fog is said to "burn off." Fog in the mountains is no reason to postpone a visit. The woods can have a unique beauty in the fog (Figure 89).

An often-asked question in the valley is, "Did it snow in the mountains?" Sometimes, during winter, a cold rain or sleet will fall in the valley, but the temperature will be low enough at the higher mountain elevations to cause snow.

Figure 89. The woods in the clouds, near Thurmont Vista Trail parking area, at elevation 1,300 feet.

Temperature Increase

It is now well known that the 1980s were the hottest decade on record since 1860, when weather data began being recorded. Many scientists believe that this increase may be evidence of a sustained global warming. Indeed, on some 100+ degree days in Washington and Baltimore during the late 1980s, the relief from the heat in the Catoctins was only relative, with temperatures there being in the 90s.

Environmental Problems

Acid Rain

For many years the American east and northeast have been receiving precipitation of relatively high acidity. The precipitation that falls on the two parks is among the most acidic to be found in the nation.

Acidity is measured on the pH scale, from 0 to 14, with 7.0 being neutral. Numbers lower than 7.0 indicate acidity; those higher than 7.0 indicate alkalinity. Natural, unpolluted rainfall is slightly acidic, with a pH of about 5.6, but during the 1980s and early 1990s precipitation in the parks averaged a pH of 4.2. Because of the exponential nature of the pH scale, this value indicates an acidity 25 times that of unpolluted precipitation.

Acid rain is created when sulfur dioxide and nitrogen oxide gases—from coal-burning power plants and industries—and nitrogen oxide gases—from vehicle exhausts—combine with moisture in the atmosphere to produce sulfuric and nitric acids. Pollutants are blown into the east and northeast by the prevailing westerly winds from the industrial midwest (Figure 90).

Although the parks have yet to experience any really devastating effects, acid rain can severely damage trees and soil processes, in addition to killing fish in streams. Extensive forest damage has already occurred in the American northeast and in Canada, where thousands of streams and lakes are devoid of fish. In Maryland, as of 1990, about 20 percent of the total stream length had acid levels dangerous to the health of fish populations.

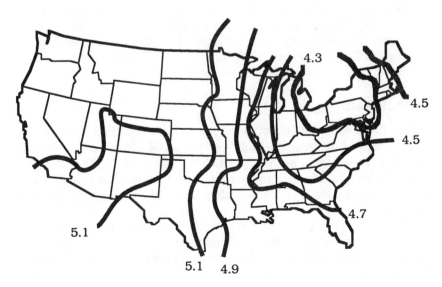

Figure 90. Average annual pH of precipitation (NADP, 1986).

Since 1982, the US Geological Survey has monitored precipitation and streamwater in the two parks. As noted above, precipitation has averaged a pH of 4.2; the lowest pH value recorded during that time was 2.96. Streamwater pH varied widely, however, ranging from 4.5 to 8.5. Different buffering, or neutralizing, conditions are responsible for this variation. These include seasonal biological processes, flow conditions, soil type, topography and, most importantly, underlying bedrock. The quartzite bedrock of the eastern parts of the parks is a poor neutralizer, while the metabasalt of the western sections is a good one; thus, it might be expected that the acid precipitation falling in the western areas tends to be neutralized or even made alkaline as groundwater and runoff, whereas that falling on the eastern, quartzite areas tends to remain acidic.

Park officials are concerned about this problem because the buffering capabilities that do exist may be finite, and at some time in the future the waters could become more acidic.

Ozone Air Pollution

Ozone, an oxygen gas with three atoms instead of the two found in regular molecular oxygen, exists in a layer in the earth's stratosphere, some 6 to 15 miles above the ground. There it acts as a shield against much of the ultraviolet radiation coming from the sun. For many years it has been known that this protective layer is being depleted, thus causing an increase in the harmful ultraviolet radiation reaching the earth's surface.

At ground level, however, ozone is a harmful air pollutant. When sunlight strikes already polluted air, high levels of ozone are produced near ground level. The ozone corrodes the waxy cuticle on plant leaves, allowing plant nutrients to escape. The weakened plants are susceptible to disease. In the parks during the late 1980s, purplish spots were observed on white pines, rhododendrons, and milkweed—indicators of high ground-level ozone. During the early 1990s, however, ozone was not thought to be a problem because the spots were not present.

Global Warming

The 1980s were the hottest decade on record. The 1990s may be even hotter. Many climatologists—although not all—believe that the average overall temperature of our planet has been slowly rising. The Catoctins, long considered a refuge from the heat, may still be that, relatively speaking, but during July 1991 temperatures above 95°F were recorded in the mountains.

Global warming is believed to be caused by a marked increase in the "greenhouse gases," molecules generated by vehicles, industrial processes, and other effects of overpopulation. These gases act in the atmosphere to trap the earth's heat and prevent it from radiating into outer space. Four gases are primarily responsible:

1) carbon dioxide – mostly from burning of fossil fuels (coal, oil)

2) methane – from livestock, termite mounds, rice paddies, landfills, wetlands

3) nitrogen oxides – from vehicle and industrial emissions

4) CFC's – from refrigerants and aerosol propellants.

One possible long-term effect of global warming is the shift of precipitation and climate zones. It is certainly possible that the drought of Summer 1991 is associated with the hypothesized global warming. If the warming trend continues, the water resources and the plant and animal habitats of the Catoctins—and of many other areas—could be greatly altered.

Another possible effect of a warming climate has already been observed: the mild winters of the past decade may be one of the causes of the overpopulation of deer in Catoctin Mountain Park. Even though many deer starve during a mild winter, fewer and fewer may be dying because winters are not as harsh as they used to be.

Water Pollution

Although water emerging below Hunting Creek Dam is less turbid than water that flows into the lake, siltation of streams could be a problem if the parks are overused. Heavy foot traffic can destroy vegetation and expose bare earth to rainfall erosion. Siltation is not a problem yet, but more use of trails—some of which have been used for over 50 years—picnic areas and campgrounds might increase the amount of dirt in runoff.

Human liquid waste is well controlled in the parks by septic systems. Camp Misty Mount, the Catoctin Park offices and Visitor Center, and all facilities of the William Houck Area of Cunningham Falls Park are hooked up to the Thurmont municipal sewage system.

Recreation Activities and Information

Recreation Opportunities

A flyer available at the Visitor Center provides an excellent map that locates the following areas.

Swimming

CFSP. Two sandy beach areas are located at Hunting Creek Lake in the William Houck Area. Lifeguards are on duty from Memorial Day to Labor Day. Inflatable objects are not permitted. A snack bar is located nearby. A daily entry fee of $2.00 per person is charged for entrance to the park and access to the beach areas from Memorial Day to Labor Day. (Figure 4).

Boating

CFSP. A private craft launch area is off Catoctin Hollow Road across from the park's Administrative Office. Gasoline motors are prohibited, but electric motors of less than 1 hp or 33 lbs of thrust can be used.

Canoes and aquacycles are for rent near the swimming area. Canoes rent for $4.20 per hour, and aquacycles for $10.00 per hour.

Picnicking

CMP. The Owens Creek and Chestnut Picnic areas have rest rooms, tables, fireplaces and tables for persons with disabilities. Chestnut Picnic Area is open year round, with portable restrooms during winter months. Owens Creek Picnic Area is open from April 15 through the end of October. Other tables are scattered through the park by roads and parking areas.
CFSP. In the Houck and Manor areas are large picnic areas with tables, fireplaces, modern restrooms, and tables for persons with disabilities. A $2.00 entry fee is charged in the Houck Area on weekends in May and September, and daily from Memorial Day to Labor Day. A 30-table shelter in the Manor Area can be rented for $80.00 per day from April through October, but it must be reserved in advance.

Fishing

Lake and stream fishing are both available. Regulations vary; see pages 86 to 88.

Trails Accessible to Persons with Disabilities

CMP. Spicebush Nature Trail is an asphalt-paved path, accessible from the Chestnut Picnic Area parking area.

CFSP. The trail to Cunningham Falls is accessible from the parking lot beside Route 77.

(See pages 136 and 141 for more details on these two trails.)

Hiking

See the Trail Guide section, pages 125 to 151.

Hunting

CMP. Hunting is NOT permitted at any time, and no firearms are permitted in the park.

CFSP. Hunting is permitted only on the 3,500 acres of undeveloped wildlands in CFSP, from October 15 through February 28. A brochure with specific information should be obtained from the CFSP Administrative Office on Catoctin Hollow Road.

Horseback Riding

CMP. Approximately 6 miles of designated public horse trails are maintained in the western portion of CMP. Open during daylight hours from April 1 through December 1, these trails are accessible from the horse trailer parking area directly across from the entrance to Camp Greentop. The parking area holds up to 5 truck and trailer units. Organized groups need to apply for a special use permit to the superintendent of CMP. All riders should obtain the brochure of information and trail regulations from the Visitor Center. It is recommended that all riders have a copy of a current negative Coggins test result when entering the park.

Cross-Country Skiing

CMP. When a 3- to 4-inch base exists, excellent cross-country skiing for the beginner or intermediate is available along certain mountainous sections of park roads that are closed to vehicle traffic during winter. Snow-covered foot trails are also open to skiing. Neither roads nor trails are groomed. No equipment rental exists at the park, but cross-country skiing seminars are held at the Visitor Center during January. Because weather conditions in the mountains can change rapidly during winter, skiers are advised not to ski alone and to stop at the Visitor Center to check conditions before heading out. More information on specific trails can be obtained at the Visitor Center, where parking is available.

CFSP. The 1.7-mile road around the lake to the picnic area is closed to vehicular traffic and offers good skiing with gentle slopes. Parking is available at the lake area, which is open from noon until sunset.

Camping

CMP: Owens Creek Campground

Owens Creek Campground is located in western CMP on a wooded mountain slope near Owens Creek and one of its tributaries. There are 51 tent/trailer sites, each with picnic table and grill. The campground has flush toilets and sinks with running water but no showers. Leashed pets are permitted. The maximum trailer length is 22 feet, and there are no hookups. Sites are secured on a first-come, first-served basis. Campers should proceed directly to the campground, locate a site, and self-register. During summer and fall, the campground fills quickly. Please do not call Catoctin Mountain Park for reservations because they are not taken.

Sites are $10.00 per night, and camping is limited to 7 consecutive days and a total of 14 days per season.

The campground is open mid-April through the third weekend in November. Adjacent to the campground are a restored 19th century sawmill and Deerfield Nature Trail Loop.

CMP: Camp Misty Mount

Camp Misty Mount has rustic cabins for rent, from mid-April until the end of October. A modern restroom and shower are located near the cabins. Each cabin has beds (no linens), fire circle, grill, and picnic table. A swimming pool is available during specified hours.

Reservations can be booked at (301) 271-3140. Cabins are $35.00 per night. A lodge that sleeps 8 is available at $80.00 per night; the infirmary for $100.00 per night.

CMP: Youth Group Camping

The Poplar Grove tenting area in the western portion of CMP can be reserved for youth groups at $15.00 per night by calling the Visitor Center at (301) 663-9388. Reservations are required. The area has pit toilets, grills, tables, fire circles and water on-site. It is closed from March 1 to April 15.

CMP: Large Camps

Camp Greentop and Round Meadow, large camps with dormitory-style facilities, are available for rent. These facilities are presently used by groups such as Frederick County Schools, District of Columbia Schools and the Maryland League for the Handicapped; some dates, however, remain open. Call the CMP Administrative Office at (301) 663-9330 for details.

CFSP: William Houck Area

William Houck Area, on the wooded ridge above Hunting Creek Lake, has 5 separate sections, A-E, each with a circular drive, and a total of 148 tent/trailer sites—each with a gravel-filled base, picnic table and grill. Each section has a rest-room building with flush toilets and hot water showers. Pets are not permitted. Maximum trailer length is 22 feet, and there are no hookups. Camp store, swimming and canoe rental are all at the nearby lake, which is accessible by a paved road.

Camping is on a first-come, first-served basis, but reservations are accepted; they are recommended during summer and on weekends. Reservations can be made by calling the CFSP Administrative Office at (301) 271-7574. The campground is open from the second weekend in April to the last weekend in October. Camp sites are $12.00 per night and are limited to a total of 14 consecutive days.

CFSP: Manor Area

The Manor Area, located just off Route 15 south of Thurmont, has 31 tent/trailer sites, with facilities similar to those at the Houck Area, except that there are no store or water sports facilites.

The Manor Area campground is open year round. During the April-October season the sites are $12.00 per night. Winter camping is available here November-March at $6.00 per night, with the facilities being one water spigot and portable toilets.

Nearby: Ole Mink Farm, Inc.

This area, off Catoctin Hollow Road on Mink Farm Road, has exclusive annual leased campsites and luxury mountain cabins. (301) 271-7012.

Nearby: Crow's Nest Campground

This campground, immediately outside of the parks' eastern boundary on Route 77, just west of the Route 15 interchange, has 78 sites, 3-point hookups, a dump station, groceries, a stocked pond and separate tenting areas. It is open year round. (301) 271-7632.

Backcountry Camping:

Backcountry or back-packer camping is NOT permitted in either park.

Emergency

Call (301) 663-9343 in the event of emergencies.

Figure 91. Cunningham Falls State Park puts on an annual Maple Syrup Demonstration.

Figure 92. Horse-drawn wagon rides are a part of the Maple Syrup Demonstration activities during spring.

Programs and Events

CFSP. During summer, various interpretive programs are scheduled on a regular basis. During fall, there is a Halloween program. During the middle two weekends in March is the Maple Syrup Demonstration, which has taken place since the early 1970s. The demonstration includes syrup making and tree tapping, video presentations, pancakes and sausages, Maryland maple products and horse-drawn wagon rides (Figures 91 and 92).

CMP. A yearly Calendar of Events is available at the Visitor Center for campfire programs and for programs in cultural history, natural history and recreational skills. Although events may vary from year to year, a typical yearly calendar might include:

Winter—orienteering; cross-country ski seminars; African-American videos; women's history videos.

Spring—wildflower walks; photo seminars; fly-tying demonstrations; Earth Day events.

Summer—campfire programs at Owens Creek Campground; whiskey still program; wetlands walks; blacksmith shop demonstration; sawmill industry talk; charcoal industry walk; and programs on deer, insects, bats, gypsy moth, fungi, and tree identification.

Fall—fall color walks, whiskey still program, orienteering.

These CMP programs and events are conducted by knowledgeable park staff members and volunteers.

Environmental Education

CMP. School groups can request information about interpretive and educational programs by writing to the Chief Ranger, Catoctin Mountain Park, 6602 Foxville Road, Thurmont, Maryland 21788.

Catoctin Mountain Park Visitor Center

The Catoctin Mountain Park Visitor Center is open all year, except for winter federal holidays. The hours of operation are:

Monday–Thursday, 10:00 A.M. to 4:30 P.M.;
Friday, 10:00 A.M. to 5:00 P.M.;
Saturday and Sunday, 8:30 A.M. to 5:00 P.M.

For more information, telephone (301) 663-9388.

It is important to remember that Hunting Creek Lake and Cunningham Falls are under the administration of the state park, not Catoctin Mountain Park.

Cunningham Falls State Park

Cunningham Falls State Park does not have a visitor center. Information may be obtained at the entry station, which is open daily from Memorial Day to Labor Day and on weekends during September and May.

At other times, on weekdays from 9:00 A.M. to 4:00 P.M. the Administrative Office is open. Its telephone number is (301) 271-7574.

Figure 93. During winter, some of the hiking trails become cross-country skiing trails.

Section II

Trail Guides
and
Driving Tours

Trails

More than 25 miles of trails run through the two parks. These are available for hiking, cross-country skiing and snowshoeing; camping, however, is permitted only in campgrounds. Catoctin Park has a horse trail in its western area. Both parks have trails accessible to persons with disabilities—Cunningham Falls and Spicebush Trails. Many trails have either interpretive leaflets or descriptive signs. Other well-marked trails have steep climbs and lead to superb overlooks.

Hiking Suggestions and Precautions

1) Dress in layers that can be added or removed as body temperature changes. Long distance hikers should pack extra clothing, food and water and a first aid kit. Mountain tops are usually colder and windier than lower elevations.

2) Bring your camera and binoculars, if you wish.

3) Wear substantial shoes or boots with non-slippery soles. Many of the trails are somewhat rocky, but in most cases a good pair of running shoes will be fine if the soles are not worn too thin.

4) Rocks are slippery when wet, and most of the Catoctins have rocky slopes and numerous rock outcrops.

5) Stay on blazed trails to prevent trespassing on private land, to prevent getting lost and to prevent soil erosion.

6) Keep a sharp eye for snakes along stone fences, downed trees and logs.

7) Avoid hiking during hunting season in the wildlands of Cunningham Falls State Park, generally the area east of Catoctin Hollow Road and south of Maryland Route 77.

8) Do not drink any water from springs, streams or lakes. Nearly all "wilderness" water is now contaminated with giardia, which gives humans a serious bout of vomiting and diarrhea.

9) Wild animals can carry rabies. Avoid direct contact with wildlife, especially an animal that seems sick, sluggish or erratic in behavior. If you or your pet is bitten, wash the wound with soap and water as soon as possible, allow the wound to bleed and see a doctor or a vet immediately.

10) During summer beware of poison ivy. It is abundant in places and can grow as a climbing vine, a trailing plant, or a bush.

11) You may wish to tell someone what trail you are planning to hike and what time you expect to arrive home.

12) Allow ample time to return to your vehicle before dark—taking into account trail length and elevation, and the season of the year.

13) Respect the rights of others by leaving behind the alcohol (prohibited on all trails) and boomboxes.

14) Do not throw litter on trails. Pack out everything that you have packed in.

Despite the necessity for these many precautions, most hikers experience few problems. In fact, in many ways you may be safer in the woods than you are driving on the highway or walking in the city.

Note: The Catoctin Trail

The Catoctin Trail runs through both parks. Its full length is 27 miles, and it begins far south of the parks at the hiker parking lot in Gambrill State Park. It runs through Frederick city watershed before entering Cunningham Falls State Park. It ends north of Catoctin Mountain Park at Mount Zion Road.

Within the parks the Catoctin Trail crosses, connects or coincides with many other trails. In the accompanying trail guides, the Catoctin Trail is described in various sections, organized according to entry points at highway crossings where parking spaces are located.

The Catoctin Trail is marked with a light blue blaze on trailside trees in the two parks. A small triangle identifies it on the accompanying trail maps.

Trail Maps

The accompanying trail maps use USGS topographic maps as their base. The contour lines indicate elevation above sea level; the difference between adjacent contour lines—known as the contour interval—is twenty feet of elevation. When a trail crosses many closely spaced contour lines, it is climbing or descending a steep slope. If the contour lines are more widely separated, the area is flatter.

A figure number is indicated for each trail that is described. Many of the trail maps overlap so that the hiker can plan different link-ups and return routes. Distances can be estimated from the scale on each map. Note that the maps have different scales.

Trail maps in this book can be photocopied and placed inside a ziplock sandwich bag for easy carrying and reference in the woods. The bag protects the paper map from moisture and fraying.

Cunningham Falls State Park

Cat Rock - beginning at parking lot across Hunting Creek from
Catoctin National Park Administrative Office (Figure 94)

This trail begins by climbing through hemlocks, the evergreen trees that
are found in stream valleys and on northern slopes in the two parks. Here
also are double-sprouted trees, which are evidence of past harvesting (see
Figure 60), and a forest understory, evidence of a controlled deer population.

When the trail crosses Bear Branch—which may be dry during the summer—the forest shows tall tulip poplars, red maples and sour gum trees.
This lush area along the moist slopes adjacent to Bear Branch is similar to
a cove forest or even a swampy forest.

The understory continues to be present as the trail climbs. Ferns also
grow across large areas.

This trail links up with the one from the dam—Old Misery Trail.

Old Misery Trail to Cat Rock and Bobs Hill - from parking lot
at Hunting Creek Lake Dam (Figure 94)

From Catoctin Hollow Road, this trail climbs steadily through a forest
abundant with tulip poplar trees. Tulip trees grow in moist sites, and because the area directly above the road is a gentle slope lying below a steeper
slope, it is an area that tends to collect and hold water.

The many double-sprouted trees in this area are evidence of the tree
harvesting that took place during the decades before the land was purchased by the government. Now with two or sometimes three substantial
trunks, these trees have sprouted from the stump that was left after harvesting.

As the trail moves higher, the climb becomes steeper and the ground
rockier. Here can be seen many dead oak trees, killed 5–10 years ago when
their leaves were consumed for several seasons by gypsy moth caterpillars. There are, perhaps, more oak casualties in the state park than in the
national park, but the forest understory of the state park is richer—as is
evidenced along the trail here. Hunting is permitted through the "wildlands" sections of the state park—thereby controlling the size of the herd
here as well as motivating the deer to move north into the national park,
where they deplete the understory.

Near the top of the trail can be found the Virginia or scrub pine, which
grows in the dry, sandy soil here. On top is a flat area covered with acres of
ferns, which have excluded everything else except some small trees:
mockernut hickory, maples, birch, oaks and tulip poplar. Double-sprouted
trees are here, too, indicating that logging was not restricted to bottom
slopes.

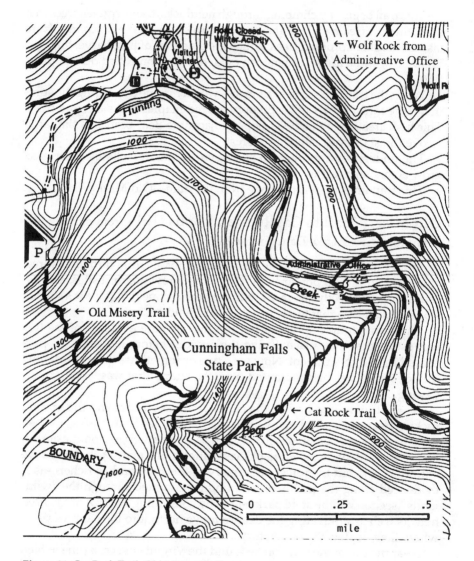

Figure 94. Cat Rock Trail, Old Misery Trail.

As the trail continues the ferns end, as if at a border, and the understory resumes. Some dogwoods can be seen, and scrub pines are present.

The trail comes to a rocky outcrop, marked by a fine, spreading American beech tree. Out on the boulder field is an excellent view of the ridge across from Hunting Creek valley, including the rock outcrop of Chimney Rock and the "saddle" in the ridge that connects to Wolf Rock (Figure 32).

Farther along but still on the flat top of this ridge is more thick understory. Sprouts of American chestnut can be seen here, sprouts that are doomed to die of the chestnut blight before arriving at maturity.

As the trail descends slightly, it again passes through a large area of ferns before it intersects with the Cat Rock Trail that comes up from Catoctin Park Administrative Office.

Turning right at the junction, the trail climbs again, passing through a power line right-of-way. As it nears the top, it passes through an area of mountain laurel, where American chestnut sprouts can also be found (Figure 95).

At this trail's highest point is the rocky outcropping of Cat Rock. Immediately to the right of the trail, the rocks can be climbed at various points

Figure 95. Young American chestnut on trail near Cat Rock.

for marvelous views to the south and west. Depending on where the rock climb is made, it can be very hazardous. The safest approach is a ramp-like path found at the far, or eastern, end of the outcrop. The Weverton quartzite that is outcropping here is a very hard rock that is highly resistant to erosion. Examples of frost wedging are all around.

The view to the south is marred by still-standing dead trees that were victims of the gypsy moth. Across the valley, which is part of the Thurmont city watershed, is another outcrop of the Weverton quartzite, the erosion-resistant, ridge-forming rock. To the east can be seen the Frederick Valley.

The northern outcrop of Cat Rock can be reached by returning to the trail at the bottom of the outcrop and by following an unmarked but well-worn path through mountain laurel to the north for about 100 feet. When the rock outcrops come into view, the trail is about 200 feet across flat rock from the edge, which provides another excellent view of Chimney Rock across the valley (Figure 32). Notice that there is less evidence of damage from the gypsy moth over in the national park, probably due to more extensive spraying.

The return trip offers a second opportunity to pass through the many different regimes and communities on this unique trail; an alternative is to follow the trail another two miles to Bobs Hill.

Bobs Hill - from Manor Area (Figure 96)

This steep, strenuous hike begins at the upper parking lot in the Manor Area. The trail follows old forest and logging roads with good footing for 1½ miles all the way up to Bobs Hill summit, where there are two overlooks.

The steep, early section of this hike is described in the Loop Hike below, but farther up, about a mile from the parking lot, the trail makes a poorly marked turn to the right from the main forest road onto a sunken road, which is probably an old logging road. In fact, before this turn it is easy to see many double-sprouted trees on the way up—evidence that logging was once done here.

After the turn, and after a brief, steep climb, beautiful mountain laurel begin to line either side of the trail. Farther up, more old logging roads can be seen intersecting from the right and the left (Figure 97). Along the main trail, near a place where one of these roads intersects, is what appears to be an old charcoal pit.

At the higher elevations are trees that have been killed by gypsy moths. When the trail begins its last sharp ascent to the summit of Bobs Hill, the passage from one member of the Weverton Formation to another member that is more resistant to erosion can be felt dramatically.

At the top are two overlooks, one to the south and one to the east. The one that faces south is on pink quartzite—evidence of iron-containing minerals. Also present are rocks that may have been wedged and cracked by frost action. Be careful climbing around on these uneven surfaces. Far below is a view of the Frederick Valley and the Triassic Border Fault that roughly divides the valley from the mountain range.

At the overlook to the east (on the other, north, side of the main trail) are large, dead trees—evidence of how quickly the gypsy moth infestation has killed trees that took decades to grow (Figure 64).

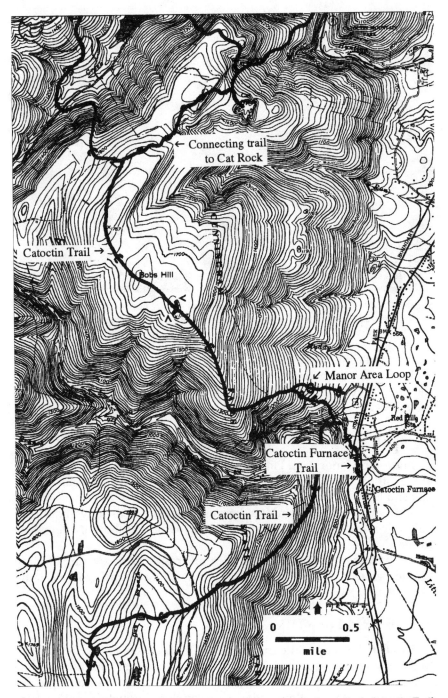

Figure 96. Bobs Hill Trail, Catoctin Furnace Trail, Manor Area Loop Trail, Catoctin Trail, Connecting trail to Cat Rock.

131

Figure 97. Old logging road off the trail to Bobs Hill. Notice how decades of erosion have caused the road to be "sunken"—a term often used for eroded dirt roads originally built in the 19th century. Trees have fallen in where none have been for a while.

The trail continues along the ridge top another two miles to Cat Rock.

Hikers should be aware that, during season, hunting is permitted in the area through which the Bobs Hill Trail passes in Cunningham Falls State Park.

Catoctin Furnace Trail (Figure 96)

From the Manor Area Picnic Grounds, this trail begins as a nice walk along Little Hunting Creek, amid American beech, sycamore, poplar, white oak and black locust.

It's a good walk for children because it is not long—only about one-half mile round trip—and it crosses over a footbridge above the four-lane Route 15.

On the other side of Route 15, the trail crosses an interesting old iron bridge before it comes to the restored ruins of Catoctin Furnace (Figure 81).

Manor Area Loop Hike (Figure 96)

Not listed on any of the trail guides or trail signs is a nice circular hike of about one mile, starting from the middle of the first parking lot in the Manor Area of Cunningham Falls State Park. Follow the trail signs for Bobs Hill/Cat Rock (yellow blaze) up a steep slope through the oak-hickory forest.

After about 0.4 mile, this trail meets the Catoctin Trail, which is marked with a blue blaze. To the right the trail climbs up to Bobs Hill. Make a turn to the left here and follow Catoctin Trail back down to the Manor Area through beautiful moss and rhododendron. Descending, the trail crosses old, sunken roads, probably used during the 19th century to haul charcoal from the mountains down to nearby Catoctin Furnace. The sinking of the roads is due to over a hundred years of water erosion.

When the trail reaches Little Hunting Creek, turn left and follow the bank of the creek to the lower picnic area. Turn left again and walk a couple of hundred yards back up the paved road to the parking lot.

Catoctin Trail - in southern section of Cunningham Falls State Park, south of Manor Area (Figure 96)

Catoctin Trail can be joined at either end of the Manor Area Loop Hike and followed south; or it can be joined by walking about a hundred feet up Little Hunting Creek from the lower Manor Area picnic area. At this point Catoctin Trail crosses Little Hunting Creek on its way south. If the creek is high, crossing might be difficult.

An alternate entry point is at a dirt parking area a few hundred feet west of the intersection of US Route 15 and Catoctin Hollow Road. The trail to the south climbs steadily up the side of the ridge and can be followed to the headwaters of Little Fishing Creek and to the City of Frederick Municipal Forest. The hiker should remember that this area is open for hunting during season.

Cunningham Falls State Park
William Houck Area/Hunting Creek Lake

Lower Falls Trail (Figure 98)

This trail parallels Hunting Creek from the lake up to Cunningham Falls. Its red blaze marking can be followed from the beach near the bathhouse; or the trail can be joined just uphill from the stone bridge on the North Beach Road, where the sign reads "Falls, ¾ mile, Lower Trail."

The trail is smooth, well-worn and well-marked. It climbs gradually up the south side of Hunting Creek valley through hemlocks and interesting deposits of metabasalt stone. It is the easier of the two trails from the lake to the falls.

Cliff Trail (Figure 98)

The Cliff Trail is the more strenuous of the two footpaths from the lake to Cunningham Falls. At the beach area, a sign behind the wishing well points to the yellow blaze of this trail (behind the Maple Syrup Demon-

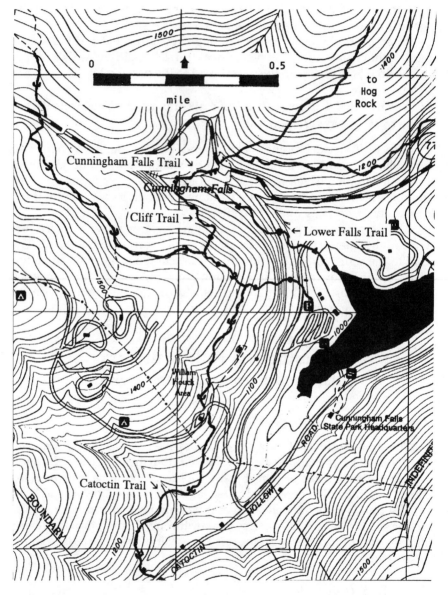

Figure 98. Lower Falls Trail, Cliff Trail, Cunningham Falls Trail (handicap accessible), and Catoctin Trail.

stration Area near the bathhouse). This trail can also be reached from its intersection with the North Beach Road (no parking) or by an access trail from the Lower Falls Trail sign mentioned above. The Cliff and Lower Falls trails are often used for up-and-back hikes to the falls from the lake.

Just above the road, the Cliff Trail begins a fairly steep climb. Above the climb, when the trail levels out, it passes large boulders of metabasalt rock. Soon the yellow blaze of the Cliff Trail is joined by the blue blaze of the long Catoctin Trail, and soon after that is the orange blaze trail, which gives access to the campground.

After a few hundred yards, the yellow blaze of the Cliff Trail turns right (north) to leave the Catoctin Trail and begin its descent to the falls. The walk down is beautiful, through boulders, hemlocks and rock escarpments, and Cunningham Falls can be heard before it is seen.

Catoctin Trail - in central Cunningham Falls State Park (Figure 98)

The lengthy Catoctin Trail can be joined at many locations in the park—for example, on the Cliff Trail, by the road to the campground near the registration building, or on Catoctin Hollow Road—but for the sake of reference, the trailhead here will be found near the bridge on Route 77 over Hunting Creek above the falls. A sign and a blue blaze point out this trail on the south side, or Cunningham Falls State Park side, of the road. Just west of the bridge guardrail is a three-vehicle parking place; the trail can be joined directly from an access path here, and it travels south.

The terrain is flat at first, and for a while the trail comes within sight of an almost level Hunting Creek, which is seen here before it begins its plunge down the falls and into the valley below. The trail then turns right and heads into the woods, paralleling an old dirt road. Along the way are beautiful hemlock trees and metabasalt greenstone with interesting quartz veins. After the hemlocks, the trail follows an old road with stone walls on each side. Next it takes a clearly marked left off the road and cuts through a rocky area with an interesting cliff and more hemlocks. To the north is the valley into which the falls plunge. Above the cliff the trail passes through still more of the beautiful hemlocks before joining the yellow blaze of the Cliff Trail.

Soon the blue-blazed Catoctin Trail takes a right and cuts along the steep slope of the mountain. This is the same steep slope on the ridge through which—farther to the north—Hunting Creek cut its valley millions of years ago.

After further descent, the trail crosses the campground road just below the registration office, and a little farther down it crosses a power line right-of-way, where metabasalt outcrops can be seen. Down the slope still farther, the trail crosses a low, flat, rocky area where several feeder streams flow down from the campground area over small falls. One of the falls resembles Cunningham Falls in miniature.

The trail continues and crosses Hauver Branch, which along with Big Hunting Creek, drains into the lake. Just after the crossing, Catoctin Trail reaches Catoctin Hollow Road, where there is a trail sign and a pull-off for parking.

Across the road, this trail climbs up the next ridge and joins the trail that connects Cat Rock and Bobs Hill.

Catoctin Trail - at Catoctin Hollow Road (Figure 98)

Two parking pull-offs provide a place to begin a hike on Catoctin Trail from the road up to the trail on top of the mountain that connects Cat Rock and Bobs Hill. It's about a mile to the top, and the climb is somewhat rocky in places but not too steep.

Along the way are excellent samples of white quartz rocks. On top, where it levels off, are mountain laurel and many trees killed by gypsy moth infestation.

Cunningham Falls Trail - accessible to persons with disabilities (Figure 98)

This trail is the easiest and most heavily used trail to the falls. It starts from the parking area off Route 77. This parking area can hold about eight cars but may be full or overflowing on busy days.

The trail is only one-third mile long and is a fairly smooth, hard-packed clay and gravel trail for its first half and a boardwalk and handrail low bridge for its second half. The view of the falls from the boardwalk is excellent.

Catoctin Mountain Park

Wolf Rock - from Wolf Rock parking lot just below Camp Misty Mount (Figure 99)

Up Park Central Road from the Visitor Center, the first parking area on the right marks the trailhead for the hike up to Wolf Rock. It begins with a climb that may be strenuous for many.

Near the top of the climb is a flat area that is good for observing the oak-hickory forest. Chestnut oak predominates here, with black oak also present. The understory includes small silver maple and mountain laurel. Just past the junction with Thurmont Vista Trail, as the descent begins, are scarlet oak, red oak and mockernut hickory.

Geologically, the trail begins in the Loudoun graywacke (dirty sandstone) conglomerate and ascends to the graywacke member of the Weverton Formation. It is difficult to determine the contact of these two formations because of the thick cover of stony soil. However, the presence of the next member of the Weverton is quite striking. A 15-foot scarp of this "ledge-maker" quartzite member of the Weverton projects from the ground and runs horizontally for several hundred feet. This is Wolf Rock, and it is an excellent example of differential erosion. The quartzite is more resistant to erosion than the adjacent graywacke sandstone. This quartzite is the rock of most of the high points in the eastern sections of the two parks: Wolf Rock and Chimney Rock in Catoctin Mountain Park; Cat Rock and Bobs Hill in Cunningham Falls State Park (Figure 100).

Be careful while climbing on Wolf Rock because the surface is broken into several deep crevasses—evidence that even this highly resistant rock is subject to erosion. Evidence of freeze-and-thaw frost wedging can be seen on sections where smaller pieces of rock are cracked and split into pieces. Different stages of breakage and separation can be observed, as can the true color of the quartzite on the freshly broken pieces.

Thurmont Vista Trail (Figure 99)

The next parking area up Park Central Road from the Visitor Center is the trailhead for the Thurmont Vista and Charcoal Trails. Thurmont Vista Trail is one of the shortest hikes to a mountaintop vista in the two parks. The path is well-worn and well-marked. The ascent is somewhat steep but not long.

Within a half-mile the trail reaches the cleared area at the top. The view to the east is of the Frederick Valley and Thurmont. It is a good place to observe the landscape that resulted from the great border fault of about 180 million years ago, when the area now occupied by the valley slid down about one mile, probably over millions of years, from the area now occupied by the mountain top.

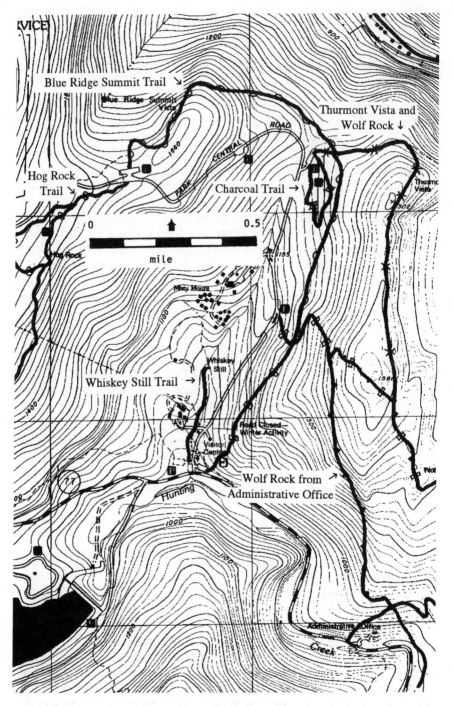

Figure 99. Wolf Rock Trail, Thurmont Vista Trail, Charcoal Trail, Hog Rock Trail, Blue Ridge Summit Trail.

From the vista the trail leads south along the ridge to the rock outcrops of Wolf Rock and Chimney Rock.

The Charcoal Trail (Figure 99)

This trail is only about one-half mile in length and is not strenuous. Trailside interpretive signs and exhibits tell the interesting history of charcoal-making in the 1800s. This is an excellent family hike (Figures 85 and 101).

Figure 100. Wolf Rock is a scarp-like, linear outcrop of the very erosion-resistant middle member of the Weverton quartzite.

Hog Rock - from Hog Rock parking lot on Park Central Road (Figure 99)

The third parking area up the mountain from the Visitor Center is the departure point for the Hog Rock and Blue Ridge Summit Vista trails. The Hog Rock Trail is self-guided; a printed interpretive guide is available at the trailhead or at the Visitor Center. The trail is entirely within the Catoctin metabasalt, and Hog Rock itself affords an excellent view to the east of the mountains of the Weverton Formation and of the gap through which Hunting Creek flows (Figure 58).

The printed guide provides excellent information on identifying trees. Notice, however, the lack of an understory in this area of the forest—evidence that the overly large deer herd has been browsing here.

Figure 101. Old charcoal pits are flat, open areas that can be seen along the Charcoal Trail or found near old logging roads in the mountains.

After the trail turns into the woods from Hog Rock for several hundred feet, to the left is an interesting flat, wet area. These are some of the headwaters of Hunting Creek; at an elevation of over 1,600 feet, these waters are near the drainage divide of Owens Creek and Hunting Creek. In fact, Park Central Road from the Thurmont Vista parking lot to the top of the mountain runs very close to the divide, with slopes to either side facing north and south.

Blue Ridge Summit Overlook and Trail (Figure 99)

This trail leaves from the north side of the Hog Rock parking lot. It affords the shortest walk in the parks to a high vista point. With only a brief, gradual climb over a small, metabasalt scarp, the trail comes quickly to the overlook. The view, to the north, is of beautiful Harbaugh Valley. It is a very peaceful place to sit for a while.

To the west (left) is the long, steep slope of Catoctin metabasalt rising to the park's highest point, which is in an area closed to the public. The steepness and thickness of this former lava flow accounts for the drop and steepness of Cunningham Falls, which is located on the same rock formation about two miles to the southeast.

The valleys and slopes seen to the north drain into Owens Creek. On the other side of the ridge from Park Central Road, the drainage is into Big Hunting Creek.

From the vista this trail continues toward the east and eventually meets the Thurmont Vista Trail.

Spicebush Nature Trail at Chestnut Picnic Area - accessible to persons with disabilities (Figure 102)

The fourth parking area to the west of the Visitor Center on Park Central Road is the Chestnut Picnic Area. The beginning of Spicebush Nature Trail is located near the first parking spaces in the picnic area.

The trail is a little over a quarter of a mile in length and is a hard-surfaced loop with wayside signs describing the upland forest. There are rest benches along the way.

The interpretive signs describe wetland plants, forest succession, chestnut trees and the understory.

Next to the parking area and connected to the trail are two double picnic tables on paved surfaces. Each table has two wheelchair locations.

Catoctin Trail (Figure 102)

Near Chestnut Picnic Area, the Catoctin Trail can be joined for hiking either to the north or to the south. This trail is described on pages 144 and 145.

Sawmill Trail - near Owens Creek Campground entrance (Figure 102)

This short, 500 foot trail begins in a small parking area, near the entrance to Owens Creek Campground on Foxville-Deerfield Road, and leads to a reconstructed, water-powered 19th century sawmill. The trail crosses a footbridge over Owens Creek, just below the tributary creek that was tapped upstream by the water raceway as a power source for the sawmill's water wheel (Figures 78 and 103).

Interpretive signs at the sawmill describe its operation. Interpretive programs are given during the summer at the Owens Creek Campground Amphitheater, which is nearby.

Brown's Farm Environmental Study Area (Figure 102)

This circular trail of less than one-half mile departs from a parking lot in Owens Creek Picnic Area. A printed guide, available at the Visitor Center, makes this an excellent trail for groups.

The guide, keyed to numbered stops on the trail, discusses plant requirements, the food chain, historical changes in land use, forest succession, animal habitats and forest communities.

This area was a working farm until it became a part of the park during the 1930s, so it is an excellent example of the return of forest vegetation to a "disturbed" area (see pages 66 to 69).

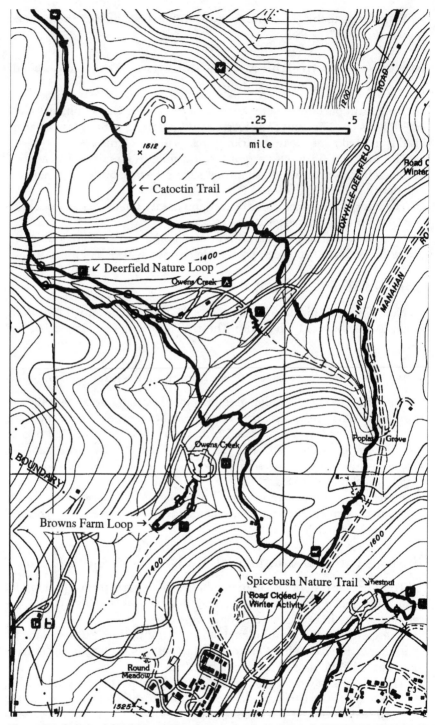

Figure 102. Spicebush Trail (accessible to persons with disabilities), Catoctin Trail, Sawmill Trail, Brown's Farm Trail, and Deerfield Nature Trail.

142

During spring, this is an excellent trail for observing wildflowers. Weekend flower walks are held here.

Deerfield Nature Trail - at Owens Creek Campground (Figure 102)

A printed interpretive guide, available at the trailhead or the Visitor Center, provides interesting information on trees, small plants, and deer browsing. Stops along the way are well marked by numbered posts. Many elms along the trail have had their bark stripped by the deer, and signs of deer browsing are present, particularly on the chewed-off branches of understory shrubs.

The forest here is denser than it is at higher elevations, and maples, elm, beech and tulip poplar are present. Down below the campground, along Owens Creek, sycamore and river birch grow.

Figure 103. Reconstructed water-powered 19th century sawmill, near Owens Creek campground.

The trail runs entirely within the Catoctin metarhyolite, a blue, brittle rock. A cross-section of the soil- and leaf-covered ground is visible from the intersection of the trail and the stream. Here all the fine material has been removed by water, leaving only a field of metarhyolite rocks.

Catoctin Trail - from Owens Creek Campground (Figure 102)

The Catoctin Trail can be picked up easily about 100 feet toward the campground from the vehicle bridge over Owens Creek. It is marked with both a blue blaze and a horseshoe, indicating that horseback riding is permitted on this section of the trail.

From this point the hiker can do either a short loop of about two miles or a long loop of about four miles. The trail begins with a steady but not steep climb through beautiful, tall trees. The understory here is thick and healthy. Along the way are outcrops of metarhyolite, some with the sharp edges that made this rock of such great use to the Indians in making arrow heads.

On top, where the trail follows an old mountain road, old stone walls built of metarhyolite can be seen. Here, at about a half-mile into the hike, a sign designates either the long loop to the right or the short loop to the left.

On the short loop, just past the sign, the trail follows the old dirt road, now sunken from decades of erosion and almost resembling a stream bed. The next left must be taken for the short loop back to Owens Creek Campground. Catoctin Trail (blue blaze and horseshoe) continues to the right and is part of the long loop.

In summer this little-used short-loop trail back to the campground may be a bit overgrown, but it is passable. Along the way can be seen the overgrown remains of a root cellar. Nearby is an area that appears to have been inhabited within the twentieth century—for it seems once to have been cleared—but it is now undergoing forest succession, with low thick brush and black locust pioneer trees.

Farther along is an old hemlock plantation. At the bottom of the slope, this trail joins the Deerfield Nature Loop Trail for return to the campground.

Catoctin Trail - from Hunting Creek bridge on Route 77 near western entrance to parks (Figure 104)

About one-half mile inside the park from the western border on Route 77, the road crosses a small bridge over Hunting Creek, just before it begins its descent down Cunningham Falls. To either side of the bridge are roadside parking places that provide easy access to Catoctin Trail.

To the south of the road, the trail leads into Cunningham Falls State Park and passes near the park's camping area. Farther on, it meets Catoctin Hollow Road.

To the north of the road the trail first passes through several hundred yards of tall hemlocks. Then the trees change quickly to deciduous, as the trail begins to climb on an old road, probably a logging road from the last century or, perhaps, a section of the original east-west road through the Catoctins. Along one stretch the trail climbs through the road, which resembles a gully with walls that are five to six feet in height—showing the erosion that has occurred since the 19th century because of water flowing off the mountain through the road bed.

Up the slope from the gully section, the trail turns to the right and leaves the old road, going into the woods. Here it parallels an escarpment of the

Catoctin metabasalt, which can be seen off the trail 100 to 200 feet to the west. The scarp can be followed to the north and the trail easily rejoined, but note that the boundary between the park and private property is just downslope several hundred feet from the bottom of the scarp.

The main trail soon crosses Park Central Road near the Chestnut Demonstration Area and Picnic Area. Here can be seen a few chestnut trees struggling to survive the blight—although they may have perished. About 100 feet to their west is a continuation of the same scarp that the trail paralleled earlier.

The return to Route 77 from the Chestnut Area can be varied toward the end. After passing through the woods and descending the old road, look for the hemlocks. Before descending into them on the trail (old road), head down through the woods and then wander through the hemlocks. Explore for springs and seeps, and follow the water into the creek along this relatively flat area. It is easy to find the way back to the parking place because traffic on Route 77 can be heard easily.

An alternative to this hike is to park at the Chestnut Picnic Area, walk down the Chestnut Demonstration Trail where it meets the Catoctin Trail, and follow it down the slope to Route 77. This approach will give the climb on the return, while the Route 77 starting point gives a hike with a descent on the return.

Hog Rock - from Cunningham Falls area and parking lot (Figure 105)

A trailhead to Hog Rock is located across Route 77 from the Cunningham Falls parking area. It is a strenuous one-mile climb up to Hog Rock, which has a view of Big Hunting Creek Valley to the east. An easier approach to Hog Rock is the interpretive trail off Park Central Road.

Cunningham Falls Nature Trail - off Hog Rock Trail (Figure 105)

The Cunningham Falls Nature Trail ends at its junction with Hog Rock trail, but it can be walked just as well from the junction down to the Visitor Center.

Cunningham Falls Nature Trail - from Visitor Center (Figure 105)

This trail begins from the parking lot across Park Central Road from the Visitor Center. The first steps of this trail are in a good place to see spring wildflowers, both along the trail and by the nearby streams.

After crossing a bridge over a small stream, the trail climbs—fairly steeply but not for too long. From there the climb is fairly gentle, and the path is well-worn and smooth.

This trail is not too far from Route 77, and traffic can be heard at times.

Interesting sights along this trail include quartz veins in greenstone, lichen-covered stones on the slopes, spring wildflowers along the trail, overturned trees with root systems visible, many chipmunks and near the

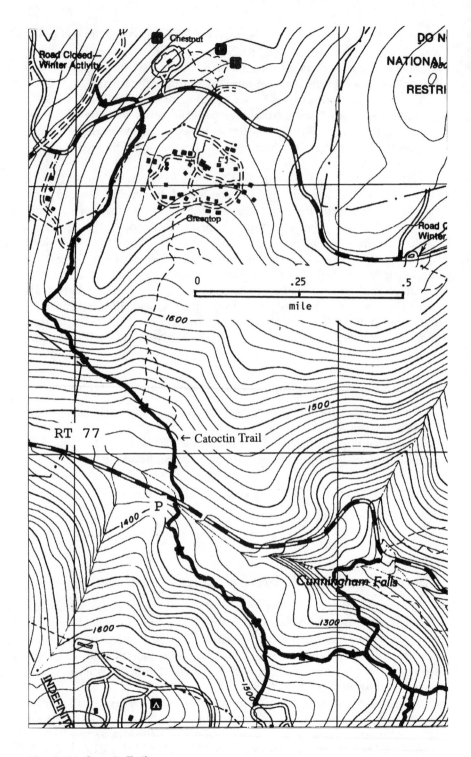

Figure 104. Catoctin Trail.

intersection of the trail and the Hog Rock Trail, a large rock outcrop with a beautiful moss covering.

Blue Blazes Whiskey Still Trail (Figure 105)

This trail begins beside the stream next to the parking lot that is across Park Central Road from the Visitor Center. It is a very easy trail to walk and is only 0.6 mile for the round trip.

The trail follows the flood plain of a tributary of Hunting Creek that is sometimes called Distillery Run. During spring months it can be a good area for seeing wildflowers.

The trail destination is a reconstructed whiskey still—a homemade, formerly illegal construction of metal kettles, barrels and pipes. It was used to distill liquor from rye or corn meal (Figure 79). Plaques at the site describe the operation and history of the still. The last still to operate in the area was shut down by law enforcement agents in July 1929.

Interpretive demonstrations are given during the summer.

Park Central Road Parallel Trail (Figure 106)

For hikers wishing to begin their hikes from the Visitor Center or to walk longer distances, a trail that generally parallels Park Central Road departs from the rear corner of the Visitor Center parking lot. A sign at that point gives trail distances: to Wolf Rock, 1.5 miles; to Chimney Rock, 2.0 miles; and to Hog Rock, 2.5 miles.

The trail is at least a tenth of a mile in the woods from the road, and noise from traffic is minimal. It climbs moderately from the Visitor Center through open woods and at various distances links up with trails to the locations listed above. Signs at these points in the woods clearly indicate directions and distances.

This trail is a good one to use in combination with others for long loop hikes.

Chimney Rock - from Camp Peniel (NPS Administrative Office) (Figure 106)

This steep climb affords interesting views of erosion associated with the Ice Age. About a half mile up the trail, after a couple of switchbacks, the trail crosses a side slope stone stream. This stone stream runs from the scarp or outcropping of rock at the top—Chimney Rock—down to Hunting Creek at the bend just below the Administrative Office (Figures 23, 24, and 107).

At Chimney Rock, cracked and split rock indicates freeze-and- thaw frost heaving, the source for the stones that were moved by periglacial solifluction almost a half mile down the slope in a stream several hundred feet wide (Figure 22). Chimney Rock is composed of the highly resistant middle member of the Weverton Formation. It affords some of the best views of the Frederick Valley and the Triassic Border Fault to the east. The outcropping rock is large enough to be clearly visible from the slope on the other side of Hunting Creek Valley.

Wolf Rock/Chimney Rock Loop Trail (Figure 106)

A loop hike of about 4 miles can begin at the Administrative Office parking lots with a trail that branches from the Chimney Rock/Wolf Rock Trail. The trail turns to the left a couple hundred yards up from the trailhead, at a sign for Park Central Road.

The trail makes a moderate ascent up a rocky slope of young trees. Along the way are ferns and mountain laurel. About a half mile up the slope are large stone fields and a scarp outcrop of quartzite of the Weverton Formation. The stone-covered slopes probably result from periglacial erosion of the scarp during Ice Age times.

Also visible here at the top of the scarp is the dip of the Weverton beds to the southeast. These beds used to arch over ten miles to the northwest and connect to the Weverton beds now visible along the top of South Mountain in Washington County—well over two hundred million years ago.

Nine-tenths of a mile from the Administrative Office the trail joins the Wolf Rock Trail that comes up from the parking lot near Camp Misty Mount. A turn to the right will lead to Wolf Rock and Chimney Rock and back to the Administrative Office. A turn to the left can lead to the Visitor Center, or the trail can simply be retraced at this point.

Crows Nest Trail - from parking lot at entrance to Catoctin
Mountain Park Administrative Office (Figure 106)

About one-quarter of a mile up the Wolf Rock/Chimney Rock Trail, the trail to Crows Nest, marked with a sign, turns to the right (south) and descends. Before the trail enters a tunnel of hemlocks, a side slope stone stream crosses from upslope (Figure 24).

The trail mostly parallels Hunting Creek and passes through the beautiful hemlocks that grow in the small flood plain. There are many places where paths lead down to Hunting Creek—usually only 50 or 100 feet away.

On the upper part is a series of jack dams that create the desirable pool-and-riffle environment that trout need for breeding. On the lower part is a natural series of pools and riffles—lovely cascades and small waterfalls plunging into clear pools. These are excellent areas for catch-and-release fishing or for just sitting or lying on a rock by the stream.

On the other side of the trail from the creek is a hillside of interesting rock ledges and huge boulders that have moved down the mountain from above.

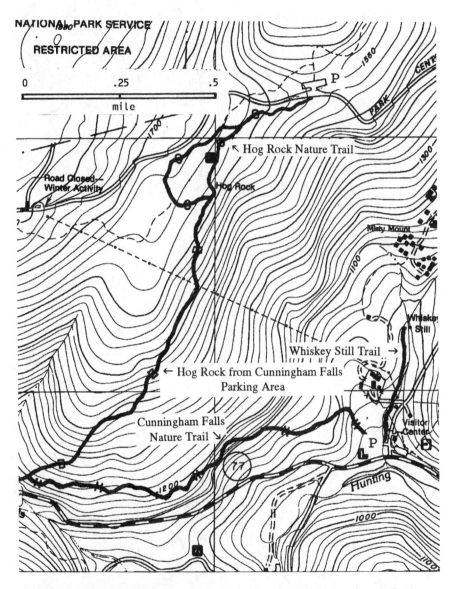

Figure 105. Hog Rock Trail and Loop from Park Central Road, Cunningham Falls Nature Trail, Whiskey Still (Blue Blazes) Trail, and Hog Rock Trail from Cunningham Falls Parking Area.

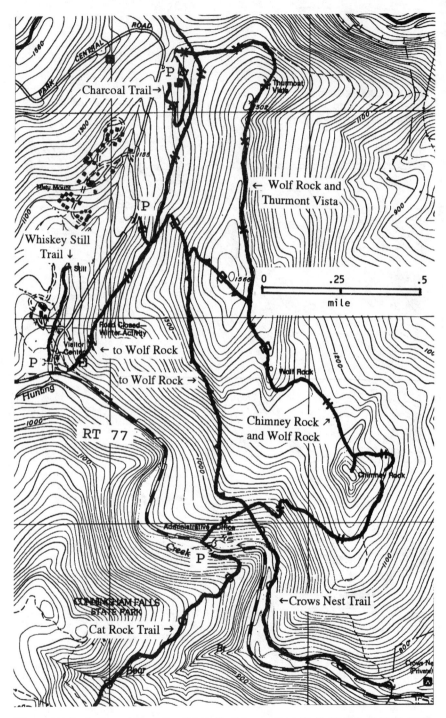

Figure 106. Park Central Road Parallel Trail, Chimney Rock Trail, Wolf Rock Trail, Wolf-Chimney Rock Loop Connecting Trail, Thurmont Vista-Wolf Rock Connecting Trail, Crows Nest Trail, Charcoal Trail, Whiskey Still Trail, and Thurmont Vista Trail.

Just past the park boundary is the private Crows Nest Campground. Please respect the "No Trespassing" signs. The Crows Nest Trail is 0.9 mile from trail head to park boundary. It is somewhat rocky in places but does not involve any long or strenuous climbs. It is a superb trail for gaining easy access to some of the most beautiful parts of Hunting Creek and to an excellent example of a stone stream.

Figure 107. Chimney Rock.

Driving Tours

The entrances to the parks used by most visitors are on Maryland Route 77:

1) From the east, Route 77 has an interchange with US Route 15 just a half-mile east of the parks.

2) From the west, Route 77 approaches from Smithsburg, which is about five miles from the park entrance.

Over 14 miles of paved roads run through the parks, and many visitors enjoy just driving through. Refer to Figure 2 or to Figure 108 for specific orientation.

Maryland Route 77 is a major through-road for traffic between the northern Hagerstown and Frederick valleys. Its scenic route generally parallels Big Hunting Creek, and it has numerous pull-offs and parking areas—the busiest of which is at Cunningham Falls.

Park Central Road travels up and through the heavily wooded mountains from the Visitor Center. Along the way are picnic areas and trailheads. Park Central Road has much less traffic than Route 77 and easily reconnects to Route 77 via Manahan Road and Foxville-Deerfield Road. Park Central Road is closed to vehicles during the winter from the Visitor Center to the top of the mountain.

The part of **Foxville-Deerfield Road** that is within Catoctin Mountain Park roughly parallels Owens Creek and passes through a wooded mountain valley. Secluded Owens Creek picnic area and campground are on this road. A loop drive can be made by connecting with Manahan Road, which is a dirt road within the park. Manahan Road is closed to vehicles during the winter. Another nice drive is to follow Foxville-Deerfield Road to Lantz (Deerfield Station) and turn right onto Maryland Route 550 for a trip down the Owens Creek valley to Route 15.

Catoctin Hollow Road travels uphill from Route 77, roughly parallel to Hunting Creek Lake and Hauver Branch. A parking area at the dam allows access to the lake or to a short walk on the dam. Farther up the road is a parking lot and boat launching area and, beyond that, the turn into the William Houck Area of Cunningham Falls State Park. Past this entrance, Catoctin Hollow Road soon leaves the park and passes by mountain residences. When it begins to descend, it parallels Little Hunting Creek. This two-lane paved road is narrow in this section, but the drive down to Route 15 is beautiful and secluded, usually with very little traffic.

Pull-Offs and Parking Spaces Along Road

For those who do not want to walk very far to see Hunting Creek, there are numerous places for parking by the road below the Visitor Center. Most of these are within 50 or 100 feet of the stream, and some might be negotiable in a wheelchair—though they are not designated as such.

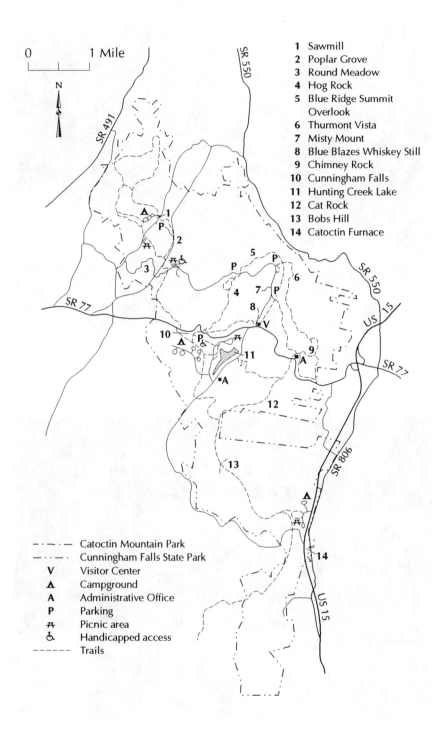

0 1 Mile

N

SR 550

SR 491

SR 77

SR 550

US 15

SR 77

SR 806

SR 15

US 15

1 Sawmill
2 Poplar Grove
3 Round Meadow
4 Hog Rock
5 Blue Ridge Summit
 Overlook
6 Thurmont Vista
7 Misty Mount
8 Blue Blazes Whiskey Still
9 Chimney Rock
10 Cunningham Falls
11 Hunting Creek Lake
12 Cat Rock
13 Bobs Hill
14 Catoctin Furnace

- — - — Catoctin Mountain Park
- — · · — · Cunningham Falls State Park
V Visitor Center
▲ Campground
A Administrative Office
P Parking
⊼ Picnic area
♿ Handicapped access
- - - - - - Trails

Figure 108. The roads of the parks.

153

Figure 109. A drive through the parks is beautiful in any season.

Figure 110. This stone stream is visible from Route 77 just below the second 90° turn below the Administrative Office.

Footpaths lead along much of both sides of the stream and provide ready access for walkers or fishermen.

An interesting stone stream, deposited by periglacial erosion associated with the Ice Age, can be found near the parking lot for the trailhead to Cat Rock. This lot is located across Hunting Creek from the entrance to the Park Administration Office. Just upstream from the upstream end of the lot, the stone stream runs up the mountain to the south. It is an excellent example of deposits left by solifluction (Figure 110).

Section III

Sources of Additional Information

Addresses for Additional Information

For information on campgrounds, facilities, interpretive programs, and other activities, contact the parks as listed below. Note: Owens Creek Campground in Catoctin Mountain Park does NOT accept reservations.

Catoctin Mountain Park
6602 Foxville Road
Thurmont, MD 21788

Phone: (301) 663-9388

Cunningham Falls State Park
14039 Catoctin Hollow Road
Thurmont, MD 21788

Phone: (301) 271-7574

For general tourist information about attractions, restaurants, accomodations and related services in the Catoctin Mountain area, contact:

Tourism Council of Frederick County, Inc.
19 East Church Street
Frederick, MD 21701-5401

Phone: 1-800-999-3613
or (301) 663-8687

or

Washington County Tourism
1826C Dual Highway
Hagerstown, MD 21740-6647

Phone: 1-800-228 STAY
or (301) 791-3130

Publications and Other Resources

Books and Journals

Geology and Geomorphology

Batten, Roger Lyman, and Robert H. Dott, Jr. 1988. *Evolution of the Earth*, Fourth Edition. New York: McGraw-Hill Book Company.

Cloos, Ernst. 1947. "Oolite Deformation in the South Mountain Fold, Maryland." Geological Society of America *Bulletin 58*: 843-918.

Cloos, Ernst. 1958. *Guidebooks 4 & 5: Structural Geology of South Mountain and Applachians in Maryland.* Baltimore: The Johns Hopkins Press.

Conners, John A. 1988. *Shenandoah National Park: An Interpretive Guide.* Blacksburg: The McDonald & Woodward Publishing Company.

Fauth, John L. 1968. *Geology of the Caledonia Park Quadrangle Area, South Mountain, Pennsylvania.* Harrisburg: Pennsylvania Geological Survey, Atlas 129a.

Fisher, George W., F. J. Pettijohn, J. C. Reed, and Kenneth N. Weaver. 1970. *Studies of Appalachian Geology: Central and Southern.* New York: Wiley Interscience.

Gathright, Thomas M. II, 1976. Geology of the Shenandoah National Park, Virginia. Charlottesville: Virginia Division of Mineral Resources *Bulletin 86.*

Geyer, Alan R. and J. Peter Wilshussen. 1982. *Engineering Characteristics of the Rocks of Pennsylvania.* Harrisburg: Topographic and Geologic Survey.

Godfrey, Andrew E. 1975. Chemical and Physical Erosion in the South Mountain Anticlinorium, Maryland. Baltimore: Maryland Geological Survey *Information Circular 19.*

Harris, Ann G., and Esther Tuttle. 1990. *Geology of National Parks*, Fourth Edition. Dubuque: Kendall/Hunt Publishing Company.

Hatcher, Robert D., Jr., and others. 1989. "Alleghenian Orogen" Chapter 5, pp. 233-288, in Robert D. Hatcher, Jr., William A. Thomas, and George W. Viele (eds.) *The Appalachian-Ouachita Orogen in the United States. Boulder*: The Geological Society of America.

Hatcher, Robert D., Jr., and others. 1989. "Tectonic Synthesis of the US Appalachians" Chapter 14, pp. 511-535, in Robert D. Hatcher, Jr., William A. Thomas, and George W. Viele (eds.) *The Appalachian-Ouachita Orogen in the United States.* Boulder: The Geological Society of America.

Judson, Sheldon, Marvin E. Kauffman, and Don L. Leet. 1987. *Physical Geology*, Seventh Edition. Englewood Cliffs: Prentice-Hall.

Levin, Harold L. 1992. *The Earth Through Time*, Fourth Edition. Fort Worth: Saunders College Publishing.

Lutgens, Frederick K., and Edward J. Tarbuck. 1993. *The Earth: An Introduction to Physical Geology*, Fourth Edition. New York: Macmillan.

McGeary, David, and Charles C. Plummer. 1993. *Physical Geology*, Sixth Edition. Dubuque: Wm. C. Brown Publishers.

Monroe, James S., and Reed Wicander. 1989. *Historical Geology: Evolution of the Earth and Life through Time*. St. Paul: West Publishing Co.

Olson, E. C. 1990. *The Other Side of the Medal: A Paleobiologist Reflects on the Art and Serendipity of Science*. Blacksburg, VA: The McDonald & Woodward Publishing Company.

Otton, Edmond G. 1970. Geologic and Hydrologic Factors Bearing on Subsurface Storage of Liquid Wastes in Maryland. Baltimore: Maryland Geological Survey *Report of Investigations* 14.

Schmidt, Martin F., Jr. 1993. *Maryland's Geology*. Centreville: Tidewater Publishers.

Schultz, Art, and Ellen Compton-Gooding, editors. 1991. *Geologic Evolution of the Eastern United States*. Martinsville: Virginia Museum of Natural History.

Sevon, William D., and Donald L. Woodrow, editors. 1985. The Catskill Delta. Boulder: The Geological Society of America *Special Paper* 201.

Shirk, William R. 1980. *A Guide to the Geology of Southcentral Pennsylvania*. Chambersburg: Robson and Kaye.

Stanley, Steven M. 1993. *Exploring Earth and Life Through Time*. New York: W. H. Freeman and Company.

Stose, Anna J., and George W. Stose. 1946. *The Physical Features of Carroll County and Frederick County*. Baltimore: Maryland Board of Natural Resources, Department of Geology, Mines, and Water Resources.

Sullivan, Walter. 1984. *Landprints: On the Magnificent American Landscape*. New York: Time Books, The New York Times Book Company.

Van Diver, Bradford B. 1990. *Roadside Geology of Pennsylvania*. Missoula: Mountain Press Publishing Company.

Way, John H. 1986. Your Guide to the Geology of the Kings Gap Area, Cumberland County, Pennsylvania. Harrisburg: Pennsylvania Geological Survey *Environmental Geology Report 8*.

Whitaker, John C. 1955. "Geology of Catoctin Mountain, Maryland and Virginia." *Bulletin* of the Geological Society of Maryland 66(4): 435-462.

Willard, Bradford. 1962. Pennsylvania Geology Summarized. Harrisburg: Pennsylvania Geological Survey *Educational Series* Number 4.

Hydrology, Climate and Environmental Problems

Anonymous. 1985. Ground-Water and Surface-Water Data For Frederick County, Maryland. Maryland Geological Survey *Basic Data Report* Number 15.

Carpenter, David H. 1983. Characteristics of Streamflow in Maryland. Maryland Geological Survey, *Report of Investigations* Number 35.

Dunne, Thomas, and Luna B. Leopold. 1978. *Water in Environmental Planning*. New York: W. H. Freeman and Company.

Manning, John C. 1987. *Applied Principles of Hydrology*. Columbus: Merrill Publishing Company.

NADP (National Acid Precipitation Assessment Program) 1986 Report. National Resource Ecology Laboratory, Fort Collins, Colorado. December, 1986.

Strahler, Arthur N., and Alan H. Strahler. 1992. *Modern Physical Geography*, Fourth Edition. New York: John Wiley and Sons, Inc.

Trombley, Thomas J., and Linda D. Zynjuk. 1985. Hydrogeology and Water Quality of the Catoctin Mountain National Park Area. United States Geological Survey, *Water-Resources Investigations Report* 85-4241.

United States Department of Agriculture, Soil Conservation Service. 1959. *Soil Survey*, Frederick County, Maryland.

Basic Ingredients For A Trout Stream

Anonymous. No date. *Stream Improvement Guide*. Pennsylvania Fish Commission, Conservation Education Division.

Battaglia, Mark, and Daniel Jones. 1986. *A Streambank Stabilization and Management Guide for Pennsylvania Landowners*. Pennsylvania Department of Environmental Resources, Bureau of Water Resources Management.

Elliott, William D., and Richard J. Montgomery. 1994. *Investigations in Biology*, Second Edition. Lexington: D. C. Heath and Company.

Miller, Jack G., and Ron Tibbot. No date. *Fish Habitat Improvement for Streams*. Pennsylvania Fish Commission.

Rivers, Susan. 1988 and 1989. *Freshwater Fisheries Division Report*. Maryland Department of Natural Resources.

Smith, Robert L. 1966. *Ecology and Field Biology*. New York: Harper and Row.

Forests

Besley, F. W. 1916. *The Forests of Maryland*. Baltimore: Maryland State Board of Forestry.

Besley, F. W. 1922. *The Forests of Frederick County*. Baltimore: Maryland State Board of Forestry.

Brooks, Maurice. 1965. *The Appalachians*. Boston: Houghton Mifflin.

Core, Earl. 1959. *Forest Trees of West Virginia*, Fifth Edition. Charleston: Conservation Commission of West Virginia.

Catlin, David T. 1984. *A Naturalist's Blue Ridge Parkway*. Knoxville: University of Tennessee Press.

Hickey II, Charles J. 1975. *The Vascular Flora of Catoctin Mountain Park, Frederick County, Maryland*. Masters Thesis, Towson State College, Towson, Maryland.

Kricher, John C., and Gordon Morrison. 1988. *Eastern Forests: A Peterson Field Guide*. Boston: Houghton Mifflin.

Martin, Alexander C., and Herbert S. Zim. 1956. *Trees: A Guide to Familiar American Trees*. New York: Golden Press.

Petrides, George A. 1972. *A Field Guide to Trees and Shrubs*, Second Edition. Boston: Houghton Mifflin.

Human History

Anderson, Elizabeth Y. No date. *Faith in the Furnace: A History of Harriet Chapel, Catoctin Furnace, Maryland*. No publisher named.

Anonymous. 1924. "Catoctin Furnace Rich in Past; Cannon of Revolution Made There," *Frederick News* (Maryland), March 20.

Kemper, Jackson III. No date. *American Charcoal Making in the Era of the Cold-blast Furnace*. National Park Service.

Libby, Jean. 1991. *African Ironmaking Culture Among African American Ironworkers in Western Maryland, 1760–1850*. Masters Thesis, San Francisco State University, San Francisco, California.

Scharf, John Thomas. 1882. *History of Western Maryland*. Philadelphia: Everts.

Singewald, Joseph T., Jr. 1911. *Report on the Iron Ores of Maryland*. Baltimore: Maryland Geologic and Economic Survey.

Szczygiel, Bonj. 1992. *The Recreation Demonstration Area Program of the New Deal*. Masters Thesis, The Pennsylvania State University, University Park.

Thompson, Michael D. 1976. *The Iron Industry in Western Maryland*. Published by the author. Available in Western Maryland Room, Washington County Free Library, Hagerstown, Maryland.

Williams, T. J. C., and Folger McKinsey. 1967. *History of Frederick County, Maryland*. Baltimore: Regional Publishing Company.

Wireman, George W. 1969. *Gateway to the Mountains*. Hagerstown: Hagerstown Bookbinding and Printing Company.

Spring Wildflowers

Martin, Alexander C., and Herbert S. Zim. 1950. *Flowers: A Guide to Familiar American Wildflowers*. New York: Golden Press.

Means, April, and John Means. 1983. *Spring Wildflowers of Washington County, Maryland: A Photographic Notebook*. Published by the authors.

Stupka, Arthur. 1965. *Wildflowers in Color*. New York: Harper and Row.

Watts, May Theilgaard. 1955. *Flower Finder*. Berkeley: Nature Study Guild.

Maps

Blue Ridge Summit, Pennsylvania—Maryland, Quadrangle, 7.5 Minute Series (Topographic). Photorevised 1985. Reston: United States Geological Survey. Scale 1:24,000.

Catoctin Furnace, Maryland—Frederick County, Quadrangle, 7.5 Minute Series (Topographic). Photorevised 1985. Reston, Virginia: United States Geological Survey. Scale 1:24,000.

Catoctin Mountain Park, Thurmont, Maryland. 1988. Reston: Air Survey Corporation of Virginia (from United States Geological Survey quadrangles). Scale 1:12,000.

Catoctin Mountains: Catoctin Mountain Park/Cunningham Falls State Park, Maryland (flyer). United States Government Printing Office: 1989-242-345/00118. Reprint 1989.

Cleaves, Emery T., Jonathan Edwards, Jr., and John D. Glaser. 1968. *Geologic Map of Maryland*. Baltimore: Maryland Geological Survey.

Cunningham Falls State Park Trail Guide. A flyer by Maryland State Forests and Parks.

Fauth, John L. 1977. *Geologic Map of the Catoctin Furnace and Blue Ridge Summit Quadrangles*. Baltimore: Maryland Geological Survey. Scale 1:24,000.

Information Sheets and Park Documents

Anonymous. 1983–1988. *Annual Aquatic Resources Report.* Resource Management Office, Catoctin Mountain Park.

Anonymous. 1988–1990. *White-tailed Deer Research.* Resource Management Office, Catoctin Mountain Park.

Anonymous. 1992. Acid Rain and its Effects on Streamwater Quality on Catoctin Mountain, Maryland. *Water Fact Sheet,* United States Geological Survey Open-File Report 92-168.

Anonymous. No date. *Man on Catoctin Mountain.* A series of pamphlets on Catoctin Mountain history published by the National Park Service. Available in Western Maryland Room, Washington County Free Library, Hagerstown, Maryland.

Catoctin Furnace and the Manor Area of Cunningham Falls State Park: Master Plan, adopted April 1983. Annapolis: Department of Natural Resources.

Fly Fisherman's Guide to Big Hunting Creek. No date. Friends of Big Hunting Creek. Catoctin Mountain Park.

Hunting at Cunningham Falls State Park. No date. Department of Natural Resources. Cunningham Falls State Park.

Howard, John, Dan Roddy, and Becky Reddinger. 1990. *Resource Management Accomplishments (plant and wildlife projects and observations).* Resource Management Office, Catoctin Mountain Park.

Interviews and Lectures

Griffin, Sally. Park Ranger/Naturalist. Catoctin Mountain Park. *Interview,* October 22, 1993.

Howard, John. Park Ranger, Resource Management Office, Catoctin Mountain Park. *Interview,* July 1991.

Roddy, Dan. Park Ranger, Resource Management Office, Catoctin Mountain Park. *Lecture* on Deer Herd Management. Sierra Club Meeting, Frederick, Maryland, Aug. 13, 1991.

Thomas, Cyrus. 1897. *Lecture* in Frederick Historical Society Papers.

Voigt, James. Park Naturalist, Catoctin Mountain National Park. *Interview,* January 30, 1988.

Voigt, James. Resource Management Specialist, Catoctin Mountain Park. *Interview,* November 2, 1993.

Index

167